The Crucible

Arthur Miller

D1366759

insight

insight

Arthur Miller's The Crucible by Sue Tweg
Insight Study Guide series

Copyright © 2011 Insight Publications Pty Ltd

First published in 2008,
reprinted in 2010, 2011 by
Insight Publications Pty Ltd
ABN 57 005 102 983
89 Wellington Street
St Kilda VIC 3182
Australia
Tel: +61 3 9523 0044
Fax: +61 3 9523 2044
Email: books@insightpublications.com
Website: www.insightpublications.com

This edition published 2011 in the United States of America by
Insight Publications Pty Ltd, Australia.

ISBN-13: 978-1-921088-82-7

Library of Congress Control Number: 2011931351

Cover Design by The Modern Art Production Group
Cover Illustrations by The Modern Art Production Group,
istockphoto® and House Industries
Internal Design by Sarn Potter

Printed in the United States of America by Lightning Source
10 9 8 7 6 5 4 3 2 1

contents

CHARACTER MAP

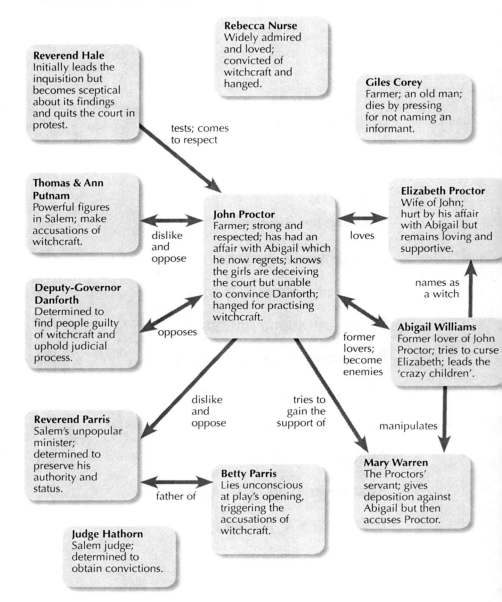

Rebecca Nurse
Widely admired and loved; convicted of witchcraft and hanged.

Reverend Hale
Initially leads the inquisition but becomes sceptical about its findings and quits the court in protest.

Giles Corey
Farmer; an old man; dies by pressing for not naming an informant.

tests; comes to respect

Thomas & Ann Putnam
Powerful figures in Salem; make accusations of witchcraft.

Elizabeth Proctor
Wife of John; hurt by his affair with Abigail but remains loving and supportive.

John Proctor
Farmer; strong and respected; has had an affair with Abigail which he now regrets; knows the girls are deceiving the court but unable to convince Danforth; hanged for practising witchcraft.

dislike and oppose

loves

names as a witch

Deputy-Governor Danforth
Determined to find people guilty of witchcraft and uphold judicial process.

opposes

former lovers; become enemies

Abigail Williams
Former lover of John Proctor; tries to curse Elizabeth; leads the 'crazy children'.

Reverend Parris
Salem's unpopular minister; determined to preserve his authority and status.

dislike and oppose

tries to gain the support of

manipulates

Betty Parris
Lies unconscious at play's opening, triggering the accusations of witchcraft.

father of

Mary Warren
The Proctors' servant; gives deposition against Abigail but then accuses Proctor.

Judge Hathorn
Salem judge; determined to obtain convictions.

OVERVIEW

About the playwright

Arthur Miller (1915–2005) was a lifelong and outspoken defender of all artists, whom he believed to have a social role to be politically critical and to challenge public ideas. He is famous for being the husband of Marilyn Monroe and a prolific writer, whose best-known plays, *Death of a Salesman* (1949) and *The Crucible* (1953), have been made into feature films.

Like Henrik Ibsen, the Norwegian playwright and social critic whose plays he admired and adapted, Miller spoke up for greater social alertness to repression. In 1987 he said:

> the arts to me represent man in his vulnerability, in his natural state, whereas politics is about power, it involves impersonations, masks, but after all the speeches are over, the plays are still there. You can't divorce them from life. (cited in Gussow 2002, p.163)

The American context in which Miller wrote is the crucial basis for our understanding of this play's universal message about the fragility of society. *The Crucible* is both a powerful dramatisation of a terrible episode of collective societal madness in seventeenth-century America, and a meditation on mid–twentieth century 'Cold War' anxieties brought on by a nuclear arms race. Miller and many of his contemporaries found themselves caught up in a witch-hunt in 1950s America when they were collectively tainted (by default, as creative artists and social critics) with treasonable Communist sympathies.

As a leftist, Miller appeared before the House Un-American Activities Committee (HUAC; see notes below) and was convicted for refusing to name alleged Communist writers. His comment that he 'could not use the name of another person and bring trouble on him' parallels situations for characters in *The Crucible* (see bbc.co.uk/onthisday for information about the HUAC charge; website details are given in the list of references at the end of this guide).

Later in life, Miller became an active president of International PEN (organisation to defend Poets', Essayists' and Novelists' rights), travelling the world with colleagues like Harold Pinter to campaign on behalf of imprisoned artists.

Synopsis

In Salem, Massachusetts, in 1692, Reverend Parris is terrified to believe that witchcraft could be the cause of his daughter Betty's comatose state. He has recently surprised a group of Salem girls, including Betty, 'dancing like heathen' in the woods at night, in rituals led by his Barbadian slave Tituba. His teenaged niece Abigail insists it was all only 'sport'. Abigail bullies the other girls to keep silent about their activities. Her sexual desire for John Proctor, and his remorse for their brief affair, are revealed. Other deep personal and community antagonism begins to emerge. Reverend Hale arrives, specifically sent for by Parris as an expert to investigate witchcraft allegations. Under pressure, Abigail shifts blame to Tituba and the tragic action begins with other girls 'naming' suspected witches.

Eight days later, John Proctor's wife, Elizabeth, tells him that a court has been convened in the Salem Meeting House. Fourteen people are in jail accused by a group of girls that is led by Abigail and includes their servant, Mary Warren. Mary Warren returns from court with a poppet (rag doll) she's made for Elizabeth, and reports that Abigail has named Elizabeth. Reverend Hale arrives to test the Proctors' religious orthodoxy. Elizabeth is arrested after Mary Warren's poppet is discovered. However, John will take Mary to court to discredit Abigail and save Elizabeth.

The credibility of Abigail's public 'performance' is dramatically demonstrated to Deputy-Governor Danforth, who sets it against the apparently conflicting testimony of the Proctors against her and Mary Warren's discredited allegations against the 'bewitched' girls. Proctor is arrested, and Hale quits the court in protest at this injustice.

Parris fears the community's hostile reaction to the hangings, especially since Abigail has fled Salem. He has been the target of anonymous threats. Rebellions against other witch trials have broken out in nearby towns. He summons Danforth to Salem on the day of execution for seven condemned witches, including Rebecca Nurse and John Proctor. Parris hopes to persuade Danforth to postpone the hangings, at least until one of the prisoners confesses to Hale, so that other executions may appear justified.

Denying Hale's plea for pardons in the absence of any life-saving confessions, Danforth stands by his interpretation of 'God's law'. He weighs the possibility of community disorder against a worse threat – that his judgement might be attacked if other sentences, already carried out, are laid open to doubt. In desperation, Hale asks Elizabeth to convince John to lie, confess and escape execution. After a loving duologue, John dictates and signs a written confession, then tears it up before Danforth can use it to make a public show. While Parris and Hale plead with Elizabeth to save her husband's life, Proctor, who has rediscovered his own 'shred of goodness', is hanged.

Character summaries

Reverend Parris: Salem's unpopular minister; supports Danforth; becomes worried about discontent in the community and finally fears for his own life.

Betty Parris: daughter to Reverend Parris; unconscious at the play's beginning; one of the girls who was dancing in the forest and who names witches.

Tituba: Parris's slave from Barbados; present with the girls when they danced and 'conjured Ruth's sisters to come out of the grave' (p.25); confesses to having seen the Devil and names Sarah Good and Goody Osburn.

Abigail Williams: Parris's seventeen-year-old niece; former servant of the Proctors and lover of John; dismissed by Elizabeth, whom she names as a witch; leads the other girls in the naming of witches; manipulates and terrifies Mary Warren by claiming to see her spirit as a 'yellow bird'; steals from Parris and leaves town when the executions begin.

Susanna Walcott: 'a nervous, hurried girl' (p.18); younger than Abigail; one of the girls who name the 'witches'.

Ann Putnam: mother to Ruth; has lost seven of eight children; blames Rebecca Nurse and accuses her of witchcraft.

Thomas Putnam: a powerful and well-off man in Salem; leads the accusations of witchcraft, motivated mainly by a desire to acquire more land.

Mercy Lewis: the Putnams' servant, 'a fat, sly, merciless girl of eighteen' (p.24); one of the girls who danced in the forest and who name the 'witches'; leaves Salem with Abigail when the executions begin.

Mary Warren: the Proctors' servant; aged seventeen; one of the girls who danced in the forest and who name the 'witches'; makes a deposition against Abigail but then, manipulated by her, accuses Proctor of being 'the Devil's man' (p.104) and begs forgiveness from Abigail.

John Proctor: farmer in his mid-thirties; respected in Salem but opposed by Parris and Putnam; has had an affair with Abigail which places pressure on his marriage to Elizabeth; persuades Mary to make a deposition against Abigail; confesses his affair to Danforth; convicted of 'sending [his] spirit out upon Mary Warren' (p.122); confesses but then tears up his confession and is hanged.

Rebecca Nurse: aged seventy-two; widely liked and admired; named as a witch and convicted of murdering the Putnams' children; refuses to confess and is hanged.

Giles Corey: a farmer; aged eighty-three; pressed to death because he will not name an informant.

Reverend John Hale: nearly forty years old; investigates the claims of witchcraft; quits the court in disgust when Proctor and Giles are arrested; realises that the convicted are actually innocent.

Elizabeth Proctor: John's wife; dismisses Abigail and is later named by her; hurt by Proctor's affair but stands by him and respects his choice not to confess publicly.

Francis Nurse: Rebecca's husband; a well-respected, prosperous farmer; attempts to save his wife with a petition, only to realise he's given the court a list of sympathisers to those who are named.

Ezekiel Cheever: a tailor who helps to carry out the court processes and tries not to think about whether they are just or not.

Marshal Herrick: a law officer with a conscience, Herrick does his duty reluctantly, especially in executing Proctor. He tries to speak up for Proctor's character (p.84), and starts drinking when he can't stand the strain of punishing neighbours and friends in Act 4.

Judge Hathorn: the judge who presides over the Salem court; has little compassion or self-doubt; convinced that the convictions and hangings are just.

Deputy-Governor Danforth: in his sixties; takes charge of the investigation; sympathises with Abigail and the girls; defends the judicial process and authority of the court; 'tests' Proctor's admission of 'lechery' by questioning Elizabeth; obtains Proctor's confession but is defeated when Proctor tears it up.

Sarah Good: a minor character; Tituba and Sarah are in jail together in Act 4, safe from hanging because they've confessed. See Mary Warren's account of Sarah Good and Goody Osburn, pp.56–8.

Hopkins: a guard in Salem jail.

BACKGROUND & CONTEXT

Written in 1953, four years after Miller's other well-known play *Death of a Salesman*, *The Crucible* has never been out of print and is performed frequently all around the world. Miller wrote that he 'can almost tell what the political situation in a country is when the play is suddenly a hit there – it is either a warning of tyranny on the way or a reminder of tyranny just past' (*Timebends*, p.348).

You need to contextualise *The Crucible* by knowing a few things about early Puritan society and about the United States in the 1950s during the Cold War. Miller repeatedly connects these two historical, social and political contexts and explores them both in the light of his own political views.

Note that from time to time in this guide I quote from Arthur Miller's autobiography, *Timebends* (1987), which provides much interesting and helpful commentary on the play and its contexts.

1950s America and the Cold War

After World War II ended with nuclear bombs a terrible reality, an arms race began between the Soviet Union (under Stalin) and the United States. Instead of a 'hot war' (with soldiers and weapons on the ground), the 'cold war' scenario played out with espionage, weapons research and aggressive diplomatic rhetoric.

F. D. Roosevelt's New Deal politics were considered 'communistic' by some conservatives, fearing radical subversive political and economic reforms. The newly-formed FBI under Hoover brought together a group of officials with their own vision of a better society, a right-wing one. The FBI worked to arouse anxieties about a foreign menace, targeting dissidents and former members of the Communist Party of America, deliberately eroding the traditional liberal tolerance of diverse views.

What resulted was a dangerous stand-off between Russian Communism and Western capitalist democratic principles.

House Un-American Activities Committee (HUAC)

The congressional committee formed in 1938 as the Dies Committee, to investigate allegations of Communist infiltration into the American administration, developed into its more sinister permanent form as HUAC in 1945. Supported by the high-profile views of Senator Joseph

McCarthy (whose name has become synonymous with 'McCarthyist' witch-hunting), HUAC was very active in the 1950s and 1960s.

It claimed to be weeding out unseen enemies of America, including Communist 'fellow-travellers' tainted simply by association. A network of informers, moles and double agents came into being, and people under interrogation were encouraged to name others.

Anyone might be suspect, including Robert Oppenheimer, the 'father of the atomic bomb', who was investigated by both the FBI and HUAC. His security clearance was revoked in 1954. Although his file apparently showed no disloyalty, Eisenhower suggested he might still be a security risk (O'Reilly 1983, pp.124–5).

Find out about the so-called 'Hollywood Seven', a group of blacklisted actors, writers and directors. Miller was also victimised and had his passport cancelled for some time. He comments on the recent film of *The Crucible*: 'there is a biting irony in this film's having been made by a Hollywood studio, something unimaginable in the fifties' (Miller 1996).

Find out about outspoken critic and broadcaster Ed Murrow, who daringly took on McCarthy in public interview. See the film *Good Night, and Good Luck*, and the website evesmag.com listed in the references at the end of this guide.

Following the Church Committee's investigation into the behaviour of the intelligence community following the Watergate scandal in 1975–6, HUAC (then called House Internal Security Committee) was finally abolished in 1975.

Kenneth O'Reilly concludes his informative book on HUAC with some important questions:

> The fundamental question – Can a democratic society tolerate a political police and remain democratic? – has been pushed aside in favour of another question: how can we be assured of an efficient and effective intelligence capability to meet the complex law enforcement problems of a modern industrial society? American political leaders today tend to prefer security and order rather than liberty. For that the FBI, along with the old House Committee on Un-American Activities and its constituency must be granted some of the credit. (O'Reilly 1983, p.296)

HUAC and *The Crucible*

The play's first audiences and critics inevitably made the connection between the Washington HUAC hearings and Salem's witch-hunt. Miller draws another sinister parallel:

> in almost every case the Committee knew in advance what they wanted the witness to give them: the names of his comrades in the [Communist] Party. The FBI had long since infiltrated the Party, and informers had long ago identified the participants in various meetings ... The main point of the hearings, precisely as in seventeenth-century Salem, was that the accused make public confession, damn his confederates as well as his Devil master, and guarantee his sterling new allegiance by breaking disgusting old vows – whereupon he was let loose to rejoin the society of extremely decent people. (*Timebends*, p.331)

KEY POINT

Miller sees both as facilitating 'rituals of guilt and confession' to appease popular anxieties aroused by disingenuous leaders in order to maintain their own power. For him, 'the same spiritual nugget lay folded within both procedures – an act of contrition done not in solemn privacy but out in the public air' (Timebends, p.331). This is the crucial resistance to authoritarian manipulation that Proctor makes at the end of the play. He refuses to hurt his innocent friends by allowing his confession to be made public just to salvage the questionable 'spiritual' authority of Danforth, Parris and Hale.

Find out about Julius and Ethel Rosenberg (executed as Communist spies):

> after one performance, upon John Proctor's execution, [the audience] stood up and remained silent for a couple of minutes, with heads bowed. The Rosenbergs were at that moment being electrocuted in Sing Sing. Some of the cast had no idea what was happening as they faced rows of bowed and silent people, and were informed in whispers by their fellows. The play then became an act of resistance for them ... (*Timebends*, p.347)

Salem 1692

Although a few miles separated village and town settlements, Salem was essentially the same group of pioneers going through a transition period into two different communities, as Miller's notes and background websites will inform you. Inevitably, disagreements about property and other rights caused ill-feeling, as did conflicting ideas about religious practice. Theocratic dominance, for example, was eroding in a farming community, especially where a minister like Parris was seen to be so unsympathetic to his parishioners' harsh realities.

Puritans and Quakers

These two breakaway groups from High Church Christianity are sometimes confused with each other. Read Miller's informative notes on the Massachusetts Puritan colony's 'autocracy by consent' (pp.15, 37–40) that became challenged by outspoken questioners like Proctor. Danforth articulates the authoritarian Puritan view, based on the Bible and Ten Commandments; but Proctor is finally driven to challenge it all as ignorance and bigotry (p.105).

Find out about the Society of Friends, or Quakers, and contrast their ideas with how Danforth, Hale and Parris approach religion. When Parris snaps at Proctor, 'What, are we Quakers?' for arguing a point (p.35), he's accusing him of adhering to a group of disrespectful free thinkers. Quakers don't have a formal paid ministry, formal liturgy, special sacraments, hymns or creeds, and their meetings are held in silence, except as members feel called to speak out loud from the 'inner light'. Ideally, Quakers look for God in every person, they engage in practical good works and social philanthropy, maintain integrity in commerce and are pacifists.

GENRE, STRUCTURE & STYLE

Genre

The genre of *The Crucible* can be discussed in several ways.

American history play

If you go to Salem, Massachusetts, you'll find a well-established theme park depicting life in seventeenth-century Puritan New England. Look up Salem interactive websites to find out more – and notice how the 'witchcraft' angle is a major attraction.

Miller's play is not so much about the reality of black arts and bad feelings, or even rivalry between the two Salem settlements in 1692, as about the social and religious conditions that prevailed at the time, which (given a sufficient episode as a catalyst) generated mass-hysteria, leading to witchcraft trials and the execution of nineteen innocent people.

Thesis play

Miller admired Ibsen for using theatre to open debates about taboo subjects and fraught relationships in the society of his time. Miller's ongoing commentary for each character and act setups are there to raise questions and guide the audience to 'read' the drama intelligently. At the centre of the play, says Miller, 'is the guilt of John Proctor, and the working out of that guilt' (cited in Gussow 2002, p.102). All his protagonists are flawed: the way they interact and affect each other is what we find interesting and moving.

Courtroom drama

Although a 'courtroom' environment is only specified for Act 3, all four acts of *The Crucible* are concerned with trying the truth of issues, testing guilt and innocence, accusations and defences, passionate arguments, questionable evidence and severe judgements. In this genre viewers are satisfied when innocent protagonists finally triumph, despite forces acting against them that maliciously threaten to pervert justice. Miller deliberately denies his audience the comfort of the generic ending.

Two key ideas relating to the courtroom drama are:

- the question of proof in witchcraft's 'invisible' crime; hence, Rebecca can be tried for 'supernatural murder', and it's very hard to disprove

- the damning 'evidence' of Elizabeth's dry eyes – women who can't weep when they're supposed to express feelings must be unnatural, and therefore guilty.

Find out about the Australian case of Lindy Chamberlain (victim of an Australian 'witch-hunt' in the 1980s) and Ruth Ellis (the last woman hanged in England; convicted of murder in 1955, she was considered 'hard' for putting on a brave face in court).

Structure

The play's story covers more than three months, from late Spring to Fall (autumn) 1692 in Salem Village. Miller deliberately constructs his action according to the classical unities of place and time, which means in each act we witness a period of continuous action in the same location on the same day.

Significantly, each of the four acts is set in a different location: read the Scene-by-Scene Analysis below to see how Miller's chosen location is of key importance to the ideas being explored in the dramatic action. To prepare for close analysis, consider now the possible significance of setting Act 1 in a girl's bedroom, Act 2 in a family kitchen, Act 3 in a Meeting House (doubling as a courtroom) and Act 4 in a prison cell.

By selecting a restricted timeframe for each act, Miller intensifies our awareness of how a day's conflicts can grow out of control. He demonstrates how interpretations of human activity escalate dangerously in a community over six months, and how interpersonal tensions break out of the intimate world of family spaces to become the subject of public theological and judicial investigation with serious punishments.

Style

The play's style is realist – that is, it looks like a 'slice of life' – but not naturalistic, a series of actions by characters. It is a play that is also a metaphor – making a larger or universal point about 'life', not just about its characters' experiences or the particular historical events in Salem in 1692. Miller said:

> I think that works of art change the consciousness of people, and their estimate of who they are and what they are and what they stand for … plays can suggest to people how to behave, how

not to behave, what is acceptable, what is unacceptable ... *The Crucible* for many people brought the consciousness of what was involved in the McCarthy period. (Gussow 2002, pp.174–5)

Language

- Listen to the rhythms and sounds of the archaic (old and no longer used) 'biblical' language used by Miller (noticed in verb/noun constructions such as 'you be', instead of our modern 'you are'; 'Let you fear nothing' whereas we would say 'Don't be afraid of anything' and so on).

- Think about the significance of the names for women – 'Goody', 'Goodwife' – a deliberately archaic form of 'wife' that carries irony, as they are in fact 'good' women, not malign witches.

Significance of the title

The word 'crucible' originally meant a night-lamp – in other words, an ancient bowl-like container for oil with a wick, made to be lit to shed light in darkness. The *Shorter OED* continues with more familiar definitions: 'a vessel, usually of earthenware, made to endure great heat, used for fusing metals, etc., a melting-pot' and also, when used metaphorically, to indicate 'any severe test or trial'. Each of these definitions resonates in *The Crucible*, a title Miller finally chose from a list which all had images of fire and burning, because he liked 'one symbolic word' that would indicate literally the burning away of impurities, which is what the play is doing' (Gussow 2002, p.185).

SCENE-BY-SCENE ANALYSIS

Although Miller doesn't divide his acts into scenes, he follows Ibsen's method of using character entrances and exits to define dramatic 'blocks of action'. As these blocks accumulate, we notice how important issues are introduced and the subtle dynamics of social and familial relationships are revealed through conversation. I've given page references in brackets to indicate the blocks: all page and line references are to the Penguin text of the play.

Act 1: an Overture

Setting: Betty's bedroom in Parris's house, Spring 1692

Scene 1 (pp.17–21)

Summary: *Parris fears his daughter Betty is the victim of witchcraft; Abigail establishes her dominance over the girls.*

Miller illustrates how the rot of suspicion leading to a witch-hunt starts to creep into Salem, fuelled by several elements, all of which are developed through Act 1:

- Tituba's pagan magic rituals for repressed impressionable girls
- Abigail's brazen lies (masking her frustrated sexual desires and revealing her narcissistic personality) to Parris, the uncle she despises and fears: note his reticence to pursue the sexual implications of dancing and nudity
- his spiritual anxiety about the Devil and witchcraft combined with self-centred terror of the social consequences of Betty's inexplicable trance state for him, Salem's minister.

Scene 2 (pp.21–5)

Summary: *Thomas and Ann Putnam enter to put more pressure on Parris.*

Ann Putnam illustrates how receptive the community is to the rot, believing absurd rumours of Betty 'flying' and eager to identify more hellish influences to explain her own daughter Ruth's sickness. Deeply unhappy, she has called on Tituba's magic to discover who murdered her seven babies.

Putnam, sensing how he can profit by stirring up the community, is keen to ascribe Salem's troubles to 'a murdering witch among us', revealed through the girls' sickness, by God's providence. Read Miller's note (pp.22–3) carefully to help you understand the undercurrents in this conversation.

Scene 3 (pp.25–7)

Summary: *Abigail, Mercy, Mary and Betty talk together.*

The girls' conversation contextualises their activities and Abigail's motives as more than 'sport'. Repressed sexual desires, lies, threats and malice are other manifestations of rot within the community.

- Abigail (aged seventeen) and Mercy (aged eighteen) agree on facts they'll confess to and be punished for by Parris.
- Mary (aged seventeen) raises the girls' anxiety by stressing widescale rumours of witchcraft, reminding them of witch-hanging in recent memory.

In a key moment, Betty (aged ten) revives briefly. The extent of the psychological pain she's bearing is expressed in her desire to 'fly' to her dead mother. She's been conscious enough to be aware of how Abigail has edited the story for Parris, and to reveal her dangerous knowledge that Abigail 'drank a charm to kill Goody Proctor' (p.26). The mood changes, and Abigail's own fears begin to build toward hysterical violence as she establishes her control over the other girls.

Q What do you think Abigail means when she threatens the girls with a 'pointy reckoning that will shudder you' and adds 'you know I can do it' (p.26)? How do they know what she's capable of?

Scene 4 (pp.27–30)

Summary: *Abigail and John Proctor talk privately and reveal their former relationship.*

Miller sees this thwarted relationship as the key motivator for the witch-hunt that follows, giving Abigail the hysterical momentum to orchestrate accusations and defensive threats.

Proctor's entry interrupts Abigail as she's beginning to dominate the other girls. They disperse with mixed feelings of attraction for and fear of him.

Notice the important change in conversational tone in this duologue, from fear and threat to light rational banter about 'mischief', what happened in the woods, the foolishness of witchcraft talk and Abigail's 'wicked' nature, which Proctor gives almost as a compliment to her. We feel we're in a different moral universe momentarily. Notice Abigail's response: she appeals to Proctor's warmth and wants to resume their relationship. He resists but she insists he has given her something better than 'hope' to wait for him.

Even Proctor's prediction that she'll be 'clapped in the stocks before [she's] twenty' (p.28) comes across as a parting joke from him. In fact, having your legs restrained in the holes of wooden planks or 'stocks' on a village green and being forced to sit there, perhaps all night, subject to jeering crowds and pelted with mud, offal and rotten fruit, or even stones, was a very humiliating and often painful public punishment for community misdemeanours. It went on well into the nineteenth century, and some stocks are still in place in English villages, like the one I grew up in. Abigail knows that if her activities are made public they could well earn her a shameful night in the stocks, or worse.

Abigail reveals her deep animosity towards Elizabeth (who dismissed her), to which Proctor (feeling guilty about his adultery and residual desire for Abigail) responds harshly. Her charge that he has 'put knowledge in [her] heart' (p.30), which he cannot take back, is the crux of the encounter. Salem's 'lying lessons' (presumably about sexual morality and sin, p.30) can't compensate for sexual pleasure she now knows.

Abigail and Proctor are interrupted by Betty's restlessness at hearing the psalm being recited (or is it something else that disturbs her, considering she can obviously hear what their conversation has been about?).

Q Does Proctor give Abigail mixed signals about his feelings for her?

Scene 5 (pp.30–7)
Summary: *Rebecca Nurse is at the centre of the conflicting group.*
From this point, goodness will become suspect as 'bewilderment' sets in among the Salem adults, a final manifestation of the pervasive moral and spiritual rot in the community that makes a witch-hunt inevitable. Rebecca and Proctor's voices put forward the last sane arguments to keep the situation rational. Notice precisely how and why Rebecca Nurse and Proctor, then Giles, antagonise Parris and the Putnams.

There are several flashpoints about different issues.

Who has healthy children?
- Rebecca (multiple mother and grandmother) appears to calm Betty effortlessly (p.32) – what has she done and how has she done it?
- Based on his own and his wife's experiences of infant deaths and conscious that 'Putnam seed have peopled this province' (p.33),

Putnam claims that children generally are dying in the village, which Proctor refutes.

- Ann Putnam's grieving envy of Rebecca's family leads her to demand to know who has killed her babies. This inevitably leads back to the suspicion that there is a 'murdering witch among us' (p.24).

Relationship of people with meeting house and minister

- Who controls the minister? Putnam directs Parris how to proceed, Proctor objects, the minister should decide after wardens are consulted.
- Why does half of the Salem village congregation stay away from church? Proctor criticises Parris for preaching about hell; Rebecca agrees (it's not good for children).
- There is a disagreement between Parris, Proctor and Giles about Parris's salary, wood allowance and ownership of the house: 'I am not used to this poverty' (p.34).
- Parris wants his status acknowledged: 'You people seem not to comprehend that a minister is the Lord's man in the parish' (p.35).
- Rebecca tries to hold the quarrelsome men together: 'you cannot break charity with your minister' (p.35).

Could there be supernatural disruption to the community?

- Parris leaps to the conclusion that his frustrations and lack of respect in the village come from the Devil: 'I cannot understand you people otherwise' (p.34).
- Spiritual factionalism charge: Proctor is accused of having a dangerous 'Quaker' idea of freedom of individual conscience, an affront to Parris as leader (p.35).

Longstanding land ownership disputes

Miller notes: 'to explain how anyone dared cry [Rebecca Nurse] out for a witch … we must look to the fields and boundaries of that time' (p.31):

- Putnam's wealth and holdings are disputed by other significant landowners Giles Corey, Proctor and Francis Nurse. It appears that he's the richest because his family are land-grabbers.
- Antagonistic landowners constantly argue over wills, writs, property transfers and unresolved claims which they are used to settling in court, never amicably.

Scene 6 (pp.37–44)

Summary: *Reverend Hale arrives to begin the inquisition.*

Notice how community bickering gives way to a much more serious inquisitorial dialogue. Hale's theatrical entry with his heavy books 'weighted with authority' (p.40), his rational 'scientific' approach in insisting on precise details rather than superstitious gossip and hearsay, combined with an earnest evangelical tone, ratchets up community anxiety about an actual supernatural threat.

Miller's extensive notes (pp.37–40) give you a broader historical perspective of 'diabolism' (discussed later in Themes). These notes underline the importance of Hale's direct role and purpose in generating the 'confession' and 'naming' panic that takes hold at the end of Act 1.

Hale leaps straight in, with what he'll later condemn as his 'bright confidence' (p.115), assessing individuals and gathering facts. Contrast his warm greeting to Rebecca Nurse, who looks 'as such a good soul should' (p.40), with his still breezy assertion that 'the justice of the court ... will send her home', after hearing about her arrest for 'supernatural murder' (pp.67–8). Remember this moment again when, doubting the court's capacity to give justice, he expresses distress at signing her death warrant (p.89), then finally accuses himself of doing 'the Devil's work' in trying to save her life by persuading her to confess to a lie – which she refuses to do (pp.114, 117).

Also compare the interest Hale shows in gathering facts about the children (Ruth Putnam cannot eat, Betty tries to fly) with his embarrassed silence at Proctor's curt remark about him being a 'sensible man'. This is why he particularly cautions Putnam against 'superstition' moments later (p.41), asserting his scientific procedural authority.

Parris pointedly introduces the community leader Putnam to Hale and is dismissive of 'farmers' Proctor and Giles Corey (inferring that their rude good health with no afflicted children already marks their sinful difference from suffering good folk).

Apparently unaware of the painful tension between Ann Putnam and Rebecca Nurse, and filing away information about dancing and conjuring spirits, Hale just notes facts: 'seven dead in childbirth', 'stoppage of prayer'. The absurd theatricality of his performance with the reference book and his description of a bodily struggle for Betty's soul overawes the group, except for Rebecca Nurse.

Note how easily individuals get caught up in the witch-hunt once it starts: Giles's question to Hale about his wife's reading and stopped prayers seems trivial compared to the main dramatic interest of the moment for Hale that Betty may fly (p.44), but it will initiate actions to hang Martha Corey and press Giles to death.

Q Does Hale have any awareness of the existing tension within this community?

Q Consider the significance of Rebecca leaving – why should they resent her? Perhaps because they know in their hearts how morally flawed they really are and why they're trying so hard to confirm that their problems are caused by witchcraft rather than something to remedy in themselves?

Scene 7 (pp.44–50)

Summary: *Accusations begin.*

This is a key scene in the play's movement towards its climax. Hale interrogates Abigail, eliciting information about dancing and the cauldron 'evidence' of Devil summoning (sufficient to convince him, corroborated by the terrified Parris). Trace how Hale maintains verbal pressure on Abigail, then Tituba, until they both collapse.

Hale inadvertently cues Abigail on how to evoke a sense of supernatural presence when he asks her about a 'sudden cold wind' (p.45). She will refer to this phenomenon in court (p.96) to initiate group hysteria. Mary Warren also later describes 'a misty coldness' of her rising hysteria that she felt before accusing Goody Osburn of bewitching her (p.57).

After denying that she's seen the Devil, Abigail tries to shake Betty awake (p.45), maybe hoping this will bring life back to normal and avert the witchcraft investigations, which would be likely to incriminate her for drinking a death charm. Note her mounting terror and her insistence she's a 'good' and 'proper' girl. Faced with Tituba (whose evidence, if heard, will condemn her), Abigail strikes first with accusations that reflect her own misdemeanours, desires and fantasies (p.46).

Hale's breakthrough moment comes when Tituba, threatened with death, breaks down, and Hale assumes she's seen the Devil. He begins a hypnotic catachism, leading her to feel safe, even privileged to be chosen as 'God's instrument' (p.48). Her vengeful fantasy on her cruel master Parris is expressed as the Devil's idea (p.48).

When Tituba names Sarah Good and Goody Osburn, then seems stuck, even when instructed by Hale to name all, Abigail protects herself by confession, followed by more naming. This cues Betty, who adds names – and the hysteria grows. Hale enjoys this moment of triumph – 'they are free!' – and Putnam sends for the law (p.49).

Q Why does Hale refuse to accept that Abigail could be telling the truth when she says 'I didn't see no Devil' (p.45)?

Q What makes Abigail and the girls snap?

Q Why are they so rapidly credited with telling the truth?

Q What do others fear? or hate? or envy? or want?

Q In Miller's 'overture', what themes have been opened for further exploration in the play? (An overture in an opera, ballet or musical is the orchestral medley of all the significant motifs and themes of the main work to follow.)

Q Are Miller's ongoing commentary notes useful? Do they help you to become involved in a dialogue about the dramatic material and ideas, rather than just being drawn into a play of characters and events?

Act II

Setting: the Proctors' living-room, eight days later (evening)

Scene 1 (pp.51–5)
Summary: John and Elizabeth discuss Abigail's role in the conflict and their own relationship.

KEY POINT

This is a brilliantly crafted scene, revealing Miller's subtle handling of intimate dialogue: the couple's tentative conversation, always teetering on the edge of argument, reveals what each person wants, fears, worries about and carries as a burden. Abigail, who has been the source of sexual and emotional tension between them, now turns out to be an even greater threat in naming Elizabeth as a witch.

The audience now receives more information, some of which reiterates Act 1 points, about the irrational kinds of 'proof' that witch trial judgements depend on: hysterical confessions of a compact with the Devil by signing one's name in blood; apparently sending a malignant 'spirit' part of yourself out of your body to attack others; mumbling (supposed curses); being unable to say prayers or the ten commandments; keeping poppets (known as 'witch dolls') stuck with pins to magically injure victims from a distance (see pp.69–71).

In spite of wanting to trust him and restore peace, Elizabeth's first question reveals her residual anxiety about John's whereabouts ... yet her immediate object is to urge him to go to Salem and reveal Abigail's fraud because she knows about Abigail's murderous activities in court. It is a difficult conversation, supported by efforts on both sides to be pleasant with food (the 'well seasoned' rabbit stew) and farm talk about crops, flowers, springtime, prosperity and their renewed relationship. They agree that Abigail's accusations are 'black mischief' (p.53).

Their bitter argument is sparked by different worries, fuelled by guilt and suspicion: John tries to think how to prove Abigail's words because they were alone, but Elizabeth thinks his delay is because he's reluctant to hurt Abigail (pp.54–5).

Q Is Elizabeth as Abigail described her to Parris in Act 1 (pp.20–1)?

Q Do you think John and Elizabeth love each other? What evidence is there at beginning of this Act?

Scene 2 (pp.55–9)
Summary: *Mary Warren returns from court with her 'poppet'.*
Elizabeth, 'perplexed' at this inappropriate gift, accepts the doll from Mary. This is taken as firm evidence of her guilt for injuring Abigail with a needle in official eyes by the end of the scene.

Proctor's sceptical response to Mary's self-justification (after the shocking description of her hysterical 'crying out' of Goody Osburn) changes abruptly when Mary reveals that she protected Elizabeth in court.

Q How has being constantly exposed to the emotionally heated environment of court affected Mary's psychological state as far as you can judge?

Q Elizabeth, thinking about what Abigail must expect, tells John: 'you have a faulty understanding of young girls' (p.60). How does her statement relate to his treatment of Mary as well in this scene?

Scene 3 (pp.59–61)

Summary: John and Elizabeth argue.

We register Elizabeth's horror – 'she wants me dead, John, you know it!' (p.59) – colliding with John's attempt to stay rational, despite feeling compromised and guilty about Abigail. The same argument about honesty and deceit flares up again.

Elizabeth knows Abigail is taking a risk to attack 'a farmer's wife' with standing in Salem (remember Parris characterising Proctor as an outspoken leader of critics to Hale), so Abigail must anticipate a 'monstrous profit in it' (p.60).

John wants to protect his wife, but how? His conflict is within: between his shame for his sexual sin (that's driving Abigail's vengeance), and his desire to restore his good name. Both are expressed as anger, aimed at himself and at Elizabeth, for articulating the kind of 'promise made in any bed'. He rejects it so vehemently because it was just about lust, 'the promise that a stallion gives a mare' (p.61), yet John perceives that in Elizabeth's eyes 'it speaks deceit, and I am honest! ... I see now your spirit twists around the single error of my life, and I will never tear it free!' (p.61).

Q Do you think that community respect would normally be sufficient protection for someone against malicious personal accusations?

Q Is Elizabeth right to believe that Abigail still 'has an arrow in' John (p.61)?

Scene 4 (pp.61–7)

Summary: Reverend Hale arrives.

In a comical moment (which immediately switches to a note of tension), Hale appears to just materialise out of the air while John and Elizabeth are slugging it out verbally. We note his presumption to walk into their home, disturbing them at night to assess 'the Christian characters of this house' (p.62). The interrogator's fear-inducing methods are illustrated, even though the stage direction (p.61) suggests Hale's initial righteous confidence is being stretched by the apparent magnitude of the Devil's attack revealed in court, with 'too much evidence now to deny it' (p.62).

Proctor is obviously appalled to think 'sensible man' Hale would suspect Rebecca Nurse (and remember his own effusive comment on her renowned goodness in Act 1). He expresses unorthodox (for that community) religious feelings and practices, relating to church-going, praying at home, Parris's need for 'golden candlesticks' and 'cathedrals, not clapboard meetin' houses', which he helped to build (pp.63–4). This again marks Proctor as an original 'plainer' Quaker-style Christian, critical of Parris – 'I see no light of God in that man' (p.63).

There is a crucial moment as Hale is leaving: Elizabeth takes the initiative to force John to make an allegation against Abigail's truthfulness, which challenges Hale – he already has a confession from Tituba and others (pp.65–6). John gets at Hale's weak spot, his residual doubts – wouldn't you lie to save your neck? John insists that the only person who couldn't lie like that is Elizabeth (p.66 – this will be a key idea in Act 3, when Hale will at last be alert and changed enough to understand her lie).

Q How does Hale think he's helping the Proctors? Why does John resent him?

Scene 5 (pp.67–8)
Summary: *Corey and Nurse interrupt with cruel reality; Hale has a testing moment.*

Elizabeth has dared to challenge Hale to be rational. Immediately he's faced with another challenge to his theological confidence, with news of two other innocent wives arrested. He maintains faith that the court's justice and processes will free Rebecca.

Hale asserts: 'these are new times ... There is a misty plot afoot so subtle we should be criminal to cling to old respects and ancient friendships' (p.68). The intellectual Hale tries to square the 'proven' Christian belief that the Devil must be alive in Salem with his equally firm belief in judicial process to arrive at the truth and protect the innocent. He tries to elicit facts, yet meanwhile fails to be of any help to Francis Nurse and Giles Corey.

Scene 6 (pp.68–72)
Summary: *Elizabeth arrested on 'poppet' evidence.*

The community crisis intensifies as servants and friends take on an uncomfortably different status as court officials and law enforcers (Mary, Cheever, Herrick) against the farmers Nurse, Giles and Proctor and their accused wives.

Superstition weighs against reason as Cheever discovers Mary's 'poppet' needle, evidence of Abigail's apparent wounding by Elizabeth. This is ironic and frightening, as Cheever is the very 'friend' Elizabeth urged John to tell about Abigail's fraud earlier (p.54). Now Cheever is convinced Elizabeth is a witch, already guilty before the trial in his eyes. John, though, defends Elizabeth's innocence, and confronts Hale's naive belief in the court's justice (p.72).

Q How does Elizabeth's violent call to have Abigail 'ripped out of the world' (p.71) affect the listeners?

Q Why does Proctor call Hale 'Pontius Pilate' (p.72)?

Scene 7 (pp.72–7)
Summary: *Proctor confronts Hale, then Mary Warren.*
How can the truth be told and Abigail's lies revealed (courtroom drama model)? There is no answer yet, although Proctor vows he will somehow 'fall like an ocean on that court!' (p.72).

Proctor accuses Hale of cowardice (p.73) but Hale makes an important speech to turn responsibility back on Salem to look for 'cause proportionate' (p.73). Hale knows it must be either fraud (as Corey challenges him to accept) or they haven't yet uncovered the reason for God's punishment – his belief demands that the latter be the truth. Is there 'some secret blasphemy that stinks to Heaven' to account for 'God's thundering wrath' (p.73)?

John Proctor hears Hale, and thinks of his adultery as the motivating cause – he's to blame, so he will make a public confession and break Abigail's 'saintliness' (p.74) as he ruins his own reputation. Mary reveals that Abigail already has the weapon of 'lechery' to use against Proctor – but he will call her bluff and force the truth to be told: 'My wife will never die for me' (p.74).

Q What does John mean when he tells Mary 'it is a providence, and no great change; we are only what we always were, but naked now' (p.75)? Compare this speech to his earlier assertion: 'We are what we always were in Salem, but now the little crazy children are jangling the keys … and common vengeance writes the law! (p.72).

Act III

Setting: the Vestry/Courtroom antechamber (a sunny day, a week later)

Key Point

This is the most harrowing Act of the play because it illustrates the futility of individuals trying to prove their innocence when the legal process is subverted by the judges' fixed ideas about sin, guilt and punishment.

Scene 1 (pp.77–80)
Summary: *the initial struggle for the voice of reason to be heard.*
We hear Martha Corey's examination in the court offstage, interrupted by Giles. His rough ejection from the courtroom brings action violently onstage – we find ourselves in the middle of Giles's tense emotional battle for Martha's life, and are shocked to hear that Rebecca Nurse has also been condemned to death (p.79).

Note that Miller invites us to contrast the attitudes of the two judges: Hathorne is ready to arrest anyone on the slightest pretext for 'contempt', whereas Danforth appears reasonable – but too procedurally slow for Corey and Nurse, who are desperate to save their condemned wives from execution. Hale's voice of reason is interrupted and talked down if he conflicts with the way Danforth wants to go.

Martha Corey's lines are taken from the transcript of her actual trial – they show how her own words lead her into a legal trap.

Scene 2 (pp.80–6)
Summary: *John Proctor and Mary Warren enter.*
Mary's deposition is refused by Danforth. Miller's stage direction indicates Danforth 'rapidly calculating' (p.81) the fundamental threat to his – and the court's – procedural authority if Mary Warren is telling the truth. This is a key moment – if Mary is believed, then Danforth will know he has been duped by Abigail and will lose face, and Parris will be in trouble (hence his aggressive response to Proctor). Hale, though, wants Mary to be heard.

Carefully consider the exchange between Danforth and Proctor (pp.81–3): Danforth is sizing up Proctor's motives and how public Mary's evidence is (i.e. how can he repress it ...). Proctor refuses to drop charges in return for Elizabeth's stay of execution because she's found to be pregnant (p.84).

The question of whether justice can be achieved in these circumstances becomes increasingly central to the unfolding drama:

- The petition for the condemned women only leads to the 'arrest for examination' of the ninety-one innocent people who signed in good faith (p.85).
- The crux of the argument is the status of the court, which Danforth articulates (p.85).
- Proctor's telling Mary to be brave – 'Do that which is good and no harm shall come to thee' (p.86) – is extremely ironic given the real nature of this courtroom.

Scene 3 (pp.86–9)

Summary: *Giles Corey presents his deposition against Putnam.*

Giles asserts that Putnam is, in effect, killing neighbours for land, although he has no direct proof. Nor will he name his source for the story that Putnam prompted his daughter to accuse George Jacobs (an old man and a big landowner, who was later hanged on the same day as Proctor). Danforth is challenged, becoming tough on Giles by convening court in the anteroom then placing him under arrest for contempt. Proctor tries to defend the integrity of Giles not revealing the identity of his informant. Note Parris's response: 'The Devil lives on such confidences! Without confidences there could be no conspiracy' (p.88). So you mustn't have secrets.

In a key moment, Danforth and Hale clash (p.88) – about the people's prodigious fear of the court, a fear that Danforth sees as implying prodigious guilt. Danforth's fixed idea is that there's a real plot to 'topple Christ', that is, to break down their society.

Scene 4 (pp.89–96)

Summary: *Mary Warren presents her deposition.*

Mary's deposition accusing Abigail and the other girls of being liars rattles Hale, who recognises that they must have a lawyer – he trusts in the legal system. Danforth always regards Hale's interventions as casting aspersions on his 'probity' (judicial fairness). When challenged by Hathorne, Mary cannot 'faint' to order (which would prove her allegation of pretence).

Scene 5 (pp.96–101)

Summary: *Proctor seeks to discredit Abigail's testimony, but Danforth is remains sympathetic to the girls.*

This key sequence begins the movement towards the destructive climax of Act 3.

When Mary tells Danforth how she kept up pretence because he seemed to believe the girls, he challenges Abigail. Which girl is lying about seeing spirits?

A series of intense interactions begins as Danforth fails to break Abigail's credibility:

- Abigail defends herself first by threatening Danforth: 'Think you to be so mighty that the power of Hell may not turn *your* wits?' (p.96). Ironically, the play demonstrates that her question hits a truth about his character, in that his wits have already been turned (through fear of civil and spiritual breakdown in the fragile community) to look for signs of the Devil in innocent people.
- She begins a virtuoso performance, manipulating the group of girls to turn hysterically on Mary. Mary will soon join in this hysteria to protect herself: note how Danforth immediately accuses her (pp.96–7). Her life depends on getting back into Abigail's group – on the side of the accusers, not of their target.
- Having lost the possibility of using Mary's testimony to save Elizabeth, John Proctor publicly confesses his adultery to discredit Abigail as a whore and potential murderess: 'She thinks to dance with me on my wife's grave!' (p.98).
- Danforth ingeniously tests the truth of John's allegations by seeing if Elizabeth (who's incapable of lying) will confirm Abigail's bad character. Prevented from reading any cues to help her answer Danforth, Elizabeth's fatal loyalty to John makes her tell a lie, hoping to blame herself rather than confirm his lechery (pp.98–100). Unlike Hale, who understands this 'natural lie' (p.100), Danforth adheres rigidly to his belief that Proctor has lied.

Scene 6 (pp.101–5)

Summary: *Abigail seizes an opportunity.*

Abigail deflects Hale's criticism of her by intensifying the hysteria against Mary, whose threatening 'yellow bird' is apparently visible to the girls, but not to Danforth (who nonetheless believes it must be there). His terror makes him threaten Mary to confess or hang as a witch. Mary breaks down in a hysterical fit, accuses Proctor of being 'the Devil's man' and is welcomed back into the group by Abigail (p.104).

Proctor, overcome by horror of Mary's betrayal, contempt for Danforth's accusations and with nothing more to lose, damns the court for 'pulling Heaven down' (p.105). Hale, who began the play as a firm believer in the capacity of the judicial process to counteract the Devil, denounces the proceedings.

KeY PoiNt

This is the point of maximum social and personal collapse into fears, accusations – mass hysteria – failure all round.

Q Contrast the rational interjections of Proctor and Hale with Danforth's questioning, which fuels Mary's religious terror (pp.101–3). Why is Danforth so keen to get her confession? How will it help to justify him?

Q What do you think John Proctor means when he claims that Lucifer's 'filthy face' (p.105) is both his own face and Danforth's? Does he mean both men are the same?

Act IV

Setting: the Fall, Salem jail three months later (moonlight to dawn)

Scene 1 (pp.102–8)
Summary: *a cheery conversation in a cell between Herrick, Tituba and Sarah Good.*

This scene is a conversation between Tituba and Sarah Good, two broken crazy women, and Marshal Herrick, who is half-drunk to suppress his feelings of reluctance. The women expect the Devil to transport them to Barbados. Note Tituba's scorn of the Massachusetts idea of Hell: 'Devil, him be pleasure-man in Barbados, him be singin' and dancin' in Barbados. It's you folks – you riles him up 'round here; it be too cold 'round here for that Old Boy' (p.108).

Q How does the black comedy of the opening prepare us to read the rest of this grim act?

Scene 2 (pp.108–12)

Summary: *Danforth arrives.*

Danforth is expecting to witness executions, not to encounter resistance from both Parris and Hale. Worryingly, these former opponents are suddenly on the same side – what's happening?

There is more community breakdown, noted as 'great contention' (p.110) by Cheever: Parris looks mad, masterless animals wander around untended, disputes about ownership are breaking out.

Parris raises a cluster of problems: what is the status of the court's decisions to condemn if chief accuser Abigail has fled Salem? Parris anticipates riots and asks for postponement, but Hathorne insists on carrying out the court's verdict to the letter.

Scene 3 (pp.113–14)

Summary: *Hale's conflict with Danforth.*

In a key speech, Danforth responds to Hale's exhausted plea for pardons and sets out his fullest statement of merciless theocratic principles ('Now hear me ...', p.113).

Still more signs of community breakdown are noted by Hale (p.114). Danforth's response is to find a stronger justification for punishments by using Elizabeth to 'soften' Proctor into a breakthrough confession.

Q Can you understand the logic of Danforth's reasoning? Do you think it is theologically and/or legally defensible?

Scene 4 (pp.114–16)

Summary: *Elizabeth is pressured by Hale and Danforth to persuade Proctor to confess.*

Pregnancy makes Elizabeth especially vulnerable to notification of Proctor's hanging and an offer of a way out. How does she respond, hearing Hale confess his 'mistaken duty' to her in his key speech ('Let not you mistake ...', p.115)?

Danforth takes Elizabeth's reluctance to strive with John as evidence of her lack of 'wifely tenderness', condemning her lack of weeping as proof of both her 'unnatural life' and her lost soul (p.116).

Q Is Hale's motive for wanting Proctor to confess entirely selfish? How has his view of life changed since Act 1?

Q 'Have the devil dried up any tear of pity in you?' Danforth asks Elizabeth (p.116). Couldn't he ask himself the same question?

Scene 5 (pp.117–19)

Summary: *John and Elizabeth meet.*

This is a key exchange of thoughts and feelings between John and Elizabeth. Contrast this reunion with the couple meeting in their house at evening in Act 2. What has changed their behaviour to each other over three months' separation in prison? What liberates them both to make their final choices?

Scene 6 (pp.119–26)

Summary: *Proctor's temptation, confession and death.*

This is John's *psychomachia* – literally his 'battle in the soul', a term used in classical drama to show a tempted character's intense inner struggle to come to the right moral decision against a wrong but attractive, easier alternative. For John it comes down to whether he should lie and live; or stay truthful and die.

Notice that two kinds of 'confession' are happening at once because Proctor's statement has a double meaning (compare this exchange to the end of Act 3 where he equates Danforth with Lucifer):

- In answer to Danforth's question 'have you seen the Devil in your life?' (p.121) he admits it publicly, but declares 'I speak my own sins' (p.123) – that is, without incriminating anyone else.

- His confession statement targets theocracy, most specifically the 'devil' Danforth, whose merciless hypocritical spirituality and legalistic destructiveness has wrecked individual lives and social bonds in Salem. Parris and Hale dance around excitedly like junior devils, urging Danforth to let Proctor just sign the paper before sunrise.

When Proctor cries 'You will not use me!' (p.124), grabbing the Devil's contract (his signed paper) and destroying it, he actually claims control over his soul in spiritual terms. Even though he'll tell Danforth 'I have given you my soul, leave me my name!' (p.124), his resolute action, like the final struggle in a medieval drama, reinforces his soul's victory and the Devil's loss.

By simultaneously reclaiming his name as an honest individual in the secular world, John asserts his capacity to think freely and to make his own judgements, independent of theological dictates. He rejects Danforth's cruel dismissal of the idea that 'it matters nothing what she

[Rebecca Nurse] thought' (p.122), and any expectation the community might have of seeing visual proof ('Damn the village!', p.123).

The question of tears comes up again. Compare John's loving advice to Elizabeth about shedding 'no tear' (p.125) with Danforth's terrible accusation of her unnaturalness earlier (p.116).

Parris and Hale again agitate like junior devils around Elizabeth, left in the cell to listen to the drum roll that will announce John's death. Note how they tempt her with accusations of vanity and pride. Why do they both (for different reasons) need to keep Proctor alive and why is Elizabeth willing to let him die well?

Q What is John thinking of when he admits to having seen the Devil in his own life?

Q Can Danforth really believe that Proctor will be 'blessed in Heaven' for making a 'false' confession? Is Danforth aware of being hypocritical? What does he think has been achieved?

Q 'God does not need my name nailed upon the church!' claims Proctor (p.124). Then who does, and why?

Q What do you think the difference is between 'what others say' and what an individual signs to (p.124)?

Q What symbolic function do you see in the final tableau onstage, with *'the new sun ... pouring in upon [Elizabeth's] face'*?

Echoes down the corridor

At the end, Miller summarises what happened historically after the witch-hunt subsided. Consider his concluding sentence a bit further. 'To all intents and purposes, the power of theocracy in Massachusetts was broken' may be accurate in broader historical terms, but day-to-day reality often gives us a different perspective. The play itself shows how deeply ingrained and trusted the twin controlling societal forces of religion and the justice system can be in even the most intelligent and rational of minds, and how equally susceptible to manipulation the 'public mind' can become.

CHARACTERS & RELATIONSHIPS

Reverend Samuel Parris

'I have fought here three long years to bend these stiff-necked people to me ...' (p.20)

'They will howl me out of Salem for such corruption in my house.' (p.22)

'I cannot offer one proposition but there be a howling riot of argument.' (p.34)

'I am not used to this poverty; I left a thrifty business in the Barbados to serve the Lord.' (p.34)

Miller's view of Parris is that 'there is very little good to be said for him' (p.13). He's materialistic, self-absorbed and driven by selfish fears. Note his repeated self-reference in conversation with Abigail in Act 1 (they will ruin **me**, **my** enemies will bring it out, a faction that is sworn to drive **me** from **my** pulpit, **my** ministry's at stake and many more.

Because he lacks real spirituality he has no impetus to take charge and help calm the community in the early stage of the panic – when he says he'll pray (p.24), Abigail sarcastically retorts that he's already prayed long enough, he must now go down and confront village rumours. Putnam insists 'they're thirsting for your word, Mister!' (p.25). When Parris fears 'a wide opinion's running in the parish that the Devil may be among us, and I would satisfy them that they are wrong', the rational man Proctor bluntly says: 'Then let you come out and call them wrong' (p.33).

Concerned more with sidestepping blame than with being rational, Parris lets himself be led by Putnam to insist it's the Devil's work. Having been tainted by Abigail's misbehaviour, he needs to reassert his loyalty to conservative Puritanism, and defends the court procedure vigorously because the girls' accusations shift attention from him. He can be seen to be a 'good minister' instrumental in saving souls if people are condemned.

KEY POINT

Parris deeply fears the power of shared confidential discussions among individuals: 'Without confidences there could be no conspiracy' (p.88).

Parris versus Proctor

'I come to see what mischief your uncle's brewin' now.' (Proctor to Abigail, p.28)

'… this man is mischief.' (Parris of Proctor, p.80)

Being temperamentally opposed in every way, these two men are mischief to each other. Proctor despises Parris for having no 'light of God' in him and for dreaming of 'cathedrals, not clapboard meetin' houses' (p.63). Parris is terrified of Proctor's outspoken criticism of his inept ministry.

Because Proctor's name is 'weighty' in the community (p.123), Parris is desperate to have the signed confession. This, he hopes, will both 'prove' that Salem witchcraft is real and justify his course of action to a doubting community.

Reverend John Hale

'The Devil can never overcome a minister.' (p.48)

'I am a minister of the Lord, and I dare not take a life without there be a proof so immaculate no slightest qualm of conscience may doubt it.' (p.89)

'I came into this village like a bridegroom to his beloved, bearing gifts of high religion; the very crowns of holy law I brought, and what I touched with my bright confidence, it died; and where I turned the eye of my great faith, blood flowed up.' (p.115)

Hale is an interesting paradox, an intelligent person with a conscience who, despite reversing his ideas completely, cannot discard what he knows to be flawed religious principles. He remains a conflicted personality, wanting to believe in both law and theocracy but unable to square either to the reality before him.

What drives him? He signs death warrants for people he believes to be innocent and struggles to make the hearings fair, with less and less confidence in the girls' 'proof'. His crisis of conscience occurs at the end of Act 3, when he completely understands Elizabeth's loving lie.

He reluctantly agrees with Proctor that people might well confess to escape hanging. Despite increasing doubts about the legitimacy of Danforth's proceedings, all Hale can bring himself to do finally is to get the very victims he condemned to confess, encouraging them to lie (and incriminate others) to save their own lives.

Hale and Proctor

'I've heard you to be a sensible man, Mr Hale. I hope you'll leave some of it in Salem.' (Proctor, p.41)
'I would save your husband's life, for if he is taken I count myself his murderer.' (Hale, p.115)

Although initially wary of each other, Hale and Proctor come to share a similarly critical view of the court proceedings. Both place a high value on reason and on their intuitive understanding of what really drives and shapes human behaviour. When Hale tests Proctor he discovers a theological 'softness' but recognises Proctor's honesty and, increasingly, his integrity. Proctor challenges Hale's comfortable faith to the limits until it breaks down and he realises his initial preconceptions were flawed.

Judge Hathorne

'… a bitter, remorseless Salem judge.' (stage direction, p.78)
'Riot! Why at every execution I have seen naught but high satisfaction in the town.' (p.111)

Hathorne is very sensitive about the status of the court and determined to protect his own authority under Danforth. He doesn't have many lines but his role is crucial in Act 3 where it looks as though the trial will have to be abandoned when evidence of Abigail's sinful dancing (which Parris wanted kept quiet) begins to come out (pp.93–4). Seeing that Danforth is starting to have doubts, Hathorne seizes control of Mary's interrogation. By discrediting Mary's testimony he passes the advantage back to Abigail – and she takes it.

Notice his crafty questions at two key points. First, when Martha claims not to know what a witch is, he asks: 'How do you know, then, that you are not a witch?' (p.77). What reply can she make to that? Second, when he asks Mary if she could 'pretend to faint' as she claims she can (p.95), he hopes to catch her as a liar either way to discredit her deposition.

Deputy-Governor Danforth

'*Danforth is a grave man ... of some humour and sophistication that does not, however, interfere with an exact loyalty to his position and his cause.*' (stage direction, p.78)

'We burn a hot fire here; it melts down all concealment.' (p.81)

'Postponement now speaks a floundering on my part; reprieve or pardon must cast doubt upon the guilt of them that died till now. While I speak God's law, I will not crack its voice with whimpering.' (p.113)

Danforth has three major concerns. First, as instructed by the Bible, he's confident that witches exist: his duty is to identify and eradicate the Devil's agents. Notice his terror at unseen spirits Abigail claims she can see – his Christianity is also mixed with superstitious dread.

Second, as a big fish in a very small pond, he wants to defend the authority and proper procedures of his theocratic court – the 'highest court of the supreme government of this province' (p.79). He is unperturbed that people are reluctant to testify, equating their high levels of fear with guilty consciences.

Finally, he wants to avoid carrying personal blame for any perceived miscarriage of justice. He believes that his court's 'hot fire' will get to the truth, rejecting Francis Nurse's claim that the 'girls are frauds ... They are all deceiving you' (p.79), as well as Mary Warren's testimony, Proctor's accusation of Abigail and Hale's challenges.

Q Why is Danforth's 'hot fire' incapable of revealing the truth?

Danforth and Proctor

'You are combined with anti-Christ, are you not?' (Danforth to Proctor, p.105)

'I hear the boot of Lucifer, I see his filthy face! And it is my face, and yours, Danforth!' (Proctor, p.105)

Proctor is shocked by Mary's betrayal and worn down emotionally by Danforth's superstitious injustice. He claims that both of them and others in court who 'quail to bring men out of ignorance' are failing in their duty and 'God damns our kind especially' (p.105). Although we see that Proctor has genuine insight and understanding, Danforth does not – and he does not want to see it.

Ezekiel Cheever

'I am clerk of the court now, y'know.' (p.68)
'It's a pity, Ezekiel, that an honest tailor might have gone to Heaven must burn in Hell. You'll burn for this, do you know it?' (Giles, p.68)

Cheever the tailor is a solid citizen suddenly placed centre stage who justifies persecuting neighbours with a formula, 'I must do as I'm told' (p.68). His superstitious gullibility is shown by his response to the needle in Elizabeth's supposed poppet: 'I never warranted to see such proof of Hell' (p.70). Yet we remember she suggested that Proctor should confide in his friend Cheever at the outset (p.54).

Mrs Ann Putnam

'How high did she fly, how high?' (about Betty, p.21)
'You think it God's work you should never lose a child, nor grandchild either, and I bury all but one? There are wheels within wheels in this village, and fires within fires!' (to Rebecca, p.33)

Miller calls her 'a twisted soul of forty-five, a death-ridden woman, haunted by dreams' (p.21). Her Christianity is laced with superstition about flying witches and conjuring spirits – hence she's always on the lookout for devilish signs. Nobody would dare to accuse her of witchcraft, yet she admits she feels no qualms about dabbling in black arts with Tituba to fuel her vindictive suspicions.

She's devastated by the deaths of seven babies over the years, meaning there are no likely Putnam heirs to the vast family fortune. As a failed matriarch she envies Rebecca, who becomes the logical target for revenge. For Ann, her daughter Ruth's dumbness is sure proof that Tituba raised dark powers (p.24) and Betty must be bewitched if she screams at hearing 'Lord's name' in a psalm.

Thomas Putnam

'There are hurtful, vengeful spirits layin' hands on these children.' (p.23)
'... the Putnam seed have peopled this province.' (p.33)

The son of the richest man in the village and a powerful community leader, Putnam's faction wants to retain Parris against majority wishes. Miller describes his 'vindictive nature' (pp.22–3).

Note that there is documented evidence to support the idea that he manipulated the 'witchcraft scare' to grab power and (by accusations) ruin or remove rivals.

Putnam versus Giles Corey

KEY QUOTES

'Thomas Putnam is reaching out for land!' (Giles Corey's charge, p.77)

Giles Corey goes to his death by pressing for refusing to name the informant who had proof of Putnam's intentions to acquire the confiscated land of George Jacobs, who in turn was condemned after being accused by Putnam's daughter (p.87). This points to Putnam's desire to increase his land as one of the key underlying causes of the witch-hunt.

Putnam versus Proctor

KEY QUOTES

'This society will not be a bag to swing around your head, Mr Putnam.' (Proctor, p.33

With his equal weight and voice as a leader, Proctor challenges Putnam as the one responsible for bullying Parris into ignoring agreed democratic processes in the church community. Another irony emerges: Putnam appears to be the dutiful Christian, while Proctor's church attendance record is poor – yet Proctor is shown to be the practical Christian, who helped build the church and respects his community's founding principles.

Abigail Williams

KEY QUOTES

'My name is good in the village! ... Goody Proctor is a gossiping liar!' (p.21)

'A wild thing may say wild things.' (p.29)

'I never knew what pretence Salem was, I never knew the lying lessons I was taught by all these Christian women and their covenanted men! And now you bid me tear the light out of my eyes? I will not, I cannot!' (p.30)

'You drank a charm to kill John Proctor's wife!' (Betty Parris, p.26)

'Aye, now she is solemn and goes to hang people!' (Proctor about Abigail, p.93)

Miller describes Abigail as a seventeen-year-old 'strikingly beautiful girl ... with an endless capacity for dissembling' (p.18). She tells her uncle that she won't 'black [her] face' and be a slave to Salem families (p.21) when Parris wonders why she gets no work after leaving the Proctors. She won't tell him the real reason why Elizabeth threw her out.

She instigates and leads the hysterical pack of 'namers', whom she bullies into submission. Her terrible threat to bring 'a pointy reckoning' to them if they betray her reminds us that she has seen horrors as a frontier child in the Indian wars. When cornered, she is bold and desperate enough to even threaten Danforth: 'Think you to be so mighty that the power of Hell may not turn *your* wits?' (p.96) – and it terrifies him.

Abigail and John Proctor

For Miller, this sexual encounter initiates the domestic disturbance out of which the entire witch-hunt grows. Like Eve suddenly gaining knowledge in the Garden of Eden, Abigail challenges Proctor for putting 'knowledge in [her] heart' (p.30).

Abigail ('performing' her persecution by Mary) says: 'No, I cannot, I cannot stop my mouth; it's God's work I do' (p.101). Is it true, in an ironic way? Proctor is forced to sacrifice his good name in a public confession (pp.97–8), but that act enables him finally to rediscover his own sense of goodness. The only weapon he has to use against her to save Elizabeth is his preparedness to be ruined.

Q Is Proctor partly responsible for the witch-hunt – and the deaths of innocent people – because he lusted after her with no hope of return for her, and was unaware of how it would affect her emotionally?

Mary Warren

KEY QUOTES

'Witchery's a hangin' error ... We must tell the truth, Abby!' (p.26)
'It were only sport in the beginning, sir, but then the whole world cried spirits ... I only thought I saw them but I did not.' (p.96)
'You're the Devil's man!' (accusing Proctor, p.104)

Miller describes seventeen-year-old Mary as 'a subservient, naive, lonely girl' (p.25). Mercy Lewis sneers at her for her 'grand peeping courage' (p.26), yet she does find temporary courage to make a deposition when Proctor supports her. Unlike Abigail, she is characterised as a typical servant girl, leading a dull unimaginative life of work.

Mary is the weakest link in Abigail's controlled group performances – she's on the edge of hysteria from the start, easily bullied into conformity but tries to speak truthfully. She faces several problems – for instance, if she tells the truth now she has essentially admitted to deliberately lying before and that's punishable. She's also anxious to stay 'in' with Abby's group, not become their victim and be condemned for bewitching them! When Hathorne and Parris test her, Mary lacks the histrionic imagination to summon hysteria – she can't bring herself to faint on command.

Abigail punishes Mary for straying by 'seeing' a yellow bird spirit, which convinces Danforth: 'Oh, Mary, this is a black art to change your shape' (p.101). Her deposition is discredited, she becomes perplexed, then is bullied by the girls, and finally breaks down into real hysteria and turns on Proctor (which will lead to his execution – a tragic parabola).

Giles Corey

Key Quotes

'I never said my wife were a witch ... I only said she were reading books!' (p.68)
'I mentioned my wife's name once and I'll burn in hell long enough for that. I stand mute.' (p.87)
'It were a fearsome man, Giles Corey.' (Elizabeth's epitaph, p.118)

Read Miller's comments (pp.43–4) on the historical Giles and Martha Corey. The transcript of her examination by Hathorne is available on the Salem website. Whereas malice drives Abigail to name others and a fear of hanging drives Mary to name Proctor, Giles draws suspicion to Martha simply by being a garrulous 'crank' who suggests to Hale that she is reading spellbooks.

Giles himself eventually becomes a victim. His wife Martha, who denies knowing what a witch is (p.77), is heard briefly (offstage only) in Act 3. The force of her outspoken character is communicated by what others say admiringly of her, yet a false accusation over pigs (p.68) is sufficient to hang her.

Tituba

'Tituba knows how to speak to the dead ...' (Ann Putnam, p.23)

'... *as always, trouble in this house eventually lands on her back.*' (stage direction, p.17)

'You are selected, Tituba, you are chosen to help us cleanse our village.' (Hale, p.48)

'Devil, him be pleasure-man in Barbados ...' (p.108)

Parris's Barbadian slave has the ambiguous distinction of being thought psychic by the superstitious group of God-fearing Puritans. She can be consulted ... but it's sailing close to black magic.

When Tituba starts to confess under Hale's questioning (pp.45–9) she reveals her hatred of Parris in a fantasy of being tempted by the Devil to kill him (p.48). She's shocked by Abigail's pre-emptive accusation, when it was Abigail who asked her to conjure with blood (p.46). She absorbs Putnam's suggestion of Good and Osburn as likely names (p.47) which she then reveals on cue in confession (pp.48–9). Hale's kindness cues Abigail and Betty to join in, accusing themselves, corroborating her list and naming more.

Rebecca Nurse

'I hope you are not decided to go in search of loose spirits, Mr Parris.' (p.32)

'This will set us all to arguin' again in the society, and we thought to have peace this year.' (p.33)

'My wife is the very brick and mortar of the church ...' (Francis, p.67)

'... if Rebecca Nurse be tainted, then nothing's left to stop the whole green world from burning.' (Hale, p.67)

In some ways, Rebecca is set up to be cast as the archetypal 'witch' figure, a wise, seventy-two year old woman who attracts envy and resentment for being more sensible and spiritually in touch than most people. She warns Parris to stay calm: 'let us go to God for the cause of it ... Let us rather blame ourselves' (p.33), the very thing Parris wants to avoid.

Miller's note on the Nurses suggests that land disputes were the basis for naming her. Putnam prompted his daughter Ruth to name Rebecca as her psychic attacker (p.32).

The film version makes much of the gallows scene, with Rebecca leading Martha, Proctor and others in the Lord's Prayer – sure public proof that she and they are innocent of witchcraft.

Elizabeth Proctor

KEY QUOTES

'I am a good woman, I know it …' (p.66)
'She wants me dead. I knew all week it would come to this!' (p.59)
'I counted myself so plain, so poorly made, no honest love could come to me!' (p.119)

Elizabeth's strength is in her conviction that she is a good woman, which enables her to be strong in dismissing Abigail (a key initiating factor behind the witch-hunt).

Elizabeth is a dutiful but insecure wife, emotionally inhibited further by John's sexual betrayal, which only confirms her low self-esteem. Her trust returns gradually over the play, especially when John fights so hard to defend her. She tells what is known as 'a noble lie' in classical tragedy, compromising her own code of honour to save that of someone she loves. Danforth's perverse literal-mindedness strips her lie of its nobility, so that she inadvertently causes more damage than good to John's cause.

John Proctor

KEY QUOTES

'A man will not cast away his good name. You surely know that.' (p.97)
'I cannot mount the gibbet like a saint. It is a fraud. My honesty is broke, Elizabeth; I am no good man.' (p.118)

Proctor attracts girls because he's masterful and masculine, unlike most of the pious churchmen. When he sees that Abby has broken Mary and intimidated Danforth, Proctor's only recourse is to sacrifice his honour and attempt to expose her pretence (p.97). The terrible irony that follows when Elizabeth fails to confirm what he's alleged about himself and Abby is that he is condemned for something much worse than lechery.

Miller notes Proctor's troubled soul: 'He is a sinner, a sinner not only against the moral fashion of the time, but against his own vision of decent conduct' (p.27). He's an unlikely hero – intelligent about farming but not book-learned, concerned about bringing up his children with right ideas, a hardworking man, ashamed of his sensual lapse as an adulterous husband and trying to make amends.

Most significantly, he sees through the moral hypocrisy and fake piety that Parris, Hale and Danforth exemplify. Elizabeth knows 'He have his goodness now' (p.126) in daring to die for his honest name against their fraudulent spirituality.

After being concerned at the way audiences had felt overwhelming pity for his anti-hero Willy Loman (in *Death of a Salesman*) 'without seeing the ironies' in Loman's situation, Miller commented that he 'wanted in *The Crucible* not to create somebody that they would just weep over, but that would arouse anger and awareness of what the terms were of these kinds of persecutions ... they're weeping for John Proctor, but they're also seeing him' (Gussow 2002, pp.88–9).

Elizabeth and John

Key Quotes

'... I will be your only wife or no wife at all!' (Elizabeth, p.61)
'My husband is a good and righteous man.' (Elizabeth, p.100)
'She only thought to save my name!' (Proctor, p.100)

Elizabeth's suspicion after his adulterous lapse continues to blight their domestic life (pp.54–5, 59–61), although he defends her and she supports him (pp.99–100, pp.117–19). Her returned love and loyalty to John commits her to one fatal lie, thinking to preserve his honour (p.100).

They are set together by the hypocritical Danforth and spiritually desperate Hale to betray each other's honesty in Act 4. In fact, they find respectful truth for themselves and each other. He won't lie and therefore dies; she won't tell him not to lie and doesn't judge him.

Elizabeth's pregnancy
'Pleading the belly' was a common plea to save condemned women from immediate execution (they were spared until a while after the child's birth, less for the guilty mother's sake than for the innocent child who hadn't deserved execution, a point of bureaucratic delicacy).

Given their damaged relationship, it is a miracle that Elizabeth's life should be saved so naturally with John's help. The fact reinforces the couple's ongoing sexual bond, even when daily domestic life is strained. It extends a promise of new life beyond Proctor's death and sheds a glimmer of hope in the bleak wreckage of Salem society.

THEMES, IDEAS & VALUES

In a play, **themes** are present and explored through a series of situations in which characters interact. As well as knowing the storyline in detail, you need to notice what goes on between characters. This is especially important in a complex play of ideas like *The Crucible*.

An **idea** for discussion in a play comes out of thinking about a particular theme in relation to what's happening in a scene. A theme will stimulate several ideas, prompting questions to think about. Discussion of ideas makes a play like *The Crucible* more alive, complex and interesting.

Ideas about themes lead you to consider **values**. In *The Crucible*, a character's values emerge through a dramatised argument that shows their struggle to make decisions and choices.

In any group, individuals will differ in their values and their views about big life questions. These depend partly on what you've been brought up to think or believe in, and also what you are working out for yourself. For example, what is right or wrong behaviour? What personality traits seem to be most valued in a good person? How precious is life? Is honesty as valuable as courage? Does it matter if you tell lies? Should you try to support your community no matter what, but especially when you personally believe something unjust is happening?

Every society reinforces its own approved **ideology**, through messages that confirm the correctness of certain political, religious and legislative structures. Generally, people within a society learn and agree to abide by a 'consensus opinion' about ethical and moral issues and just tend to do 'the right thing' most of the time – but this can be a fragile agreement at best, especially in stressful times. Social cohesion can break down depressingly quickly when people feel threatened, for example. Can we find out how and why?

We need to keep reminding ourselves that imaginative plays and films are never just entertainment, they always carry (however lightly or unintentionally) **ideological messages** about the world. Some are more conscious of presenting a point of view that either aims to persuade us overwhelmingly or challenges us to think out things for ourselves. Creative artists like Miller believe their work offers entertainment that also gives society an imaginative way of looking at itself critically.

The Crucible makes its values clear in positively rating John Proctor's human weakness and final bravery (of which it approves) against the narrowness and self-interest of theocratic leaders, especially Parris and Danforth, who manipulate those who are anxious and/or vulnerable in society. Danforth represents the extreme voice of theocracy when he argues that public fear of his court stems from general guiltiness for sin and 'a moving plot to topple Christ in the country' (p.88). His mission is to purge Salem of that sin. Hale has a similar purpose but his reason gradually leads him to the terrible realisation that he has been part of a religious court which unjustly condemns innocent people.

Belonging

It seems to be a natural human instinct, shared by many other living creatures, to belong to a group, herd or tribe of some kind. There can be safety from predators in numbers, while nurturing and sharing can keep the group viable. But belonging to a group means obligations as well as rights, and sometimes group dynamics evolve in ways that become dangerous to individual members, or drawbacks to belonging can outweigh perceived advantages.

Some basic questions relating to this theme are: How do you establish that you belong in your community or family group? How do you gain (or risk losing) acceptance by a group? What are some reasons for being left out – and can you identify them if it happens?

Belonging to a community

Everyone is expected to demonstrate adherence to a large group – most people do this simply by following the normative patterns for the group in everyday life and obeying its laws. This idea is central to Miller's play about Salem life.

The Crucible is about a tight Christian community network bound by strict moral, legal and religious beliefs and practices in a recently established pioneer settlement. People conform more or less to the agreed rules because they want to feel the security of belonging. At the same time, all kinds of personal conflicts between individuals and family groups simmering beneath the surface are easily stirred up when a threat to the community is perceived. Then people who are already frustrated and under pressure in their personal lives look for someone to blame ... and a witch-hunt begins.

Q In the play, what are the key threats to Salem's sense of being a community? Do these threats lie outside the community or are they forces and tensions already present within the group?

The importance of fitting in

KEY QUOTES

'Your soul alone is the issue here, Mister, and you will prove its whiteness or you cannot live in a Christian country.' (Danforth to Proctor, p.122)

In his opening notes to Act 1 (p.16), Miller discusses how sadly conflicted characters like Hale struggle to belong to a community that enforces 'exclusion and prohibition'. The Massachusetts province theocracy (of which Boston, Salem, Andover and other struggling settlements were part) was founded on a noble idea, the central importance of maintaining Christian goodness and unity of purpose. In order to maintain that high ideal it became inevitable that the society *must* exclude and prohibit anything that appeared to undermine that cohesiveness – and so individuality and personal choice must submit to regulation.

Q In the play, who suffers in this process of 'exclusion and prohibition'?

Belonging with family and friends

The most intimate binding relationships people can experience are with family and friends. At best, they can offer love, security, companionship, helpful advice and criticism, protection and much more – just by being there, they also contribute to an individual's self-esteem. We derive confidence from having a defined place and people who want to be with us.

Q Look closely at the family groups and identifiable friendships in *The Crucible* – how far do they conform to the description above? What variations do you notice? How are individuals affected by being within these relationships?

Being accepted by a peer group

KEY QUOTES

'Now look you. All of you. We danced. And Tituba conjured Ruth Putnam's dead sisters. And that is all.' (Abigail, p.26)
'Abby, Abby, I'll never hurt you more!' (Mary, p.104)

Can you identify your peer-group? Is it something you can talk about or are there unspoken codes of behaviour and understanding that are just there, to which you conform without too much thought? Do you sometimes disagree with what your friendship group does or says?

The Crucible reminds us that pressures to conform to the expectations and conventions of a group can be felt equally strongly by all ages, from teenagers to the elderly.

Identify the members of some of Salem's peer groups: farmers, community officials, rich and poor, ministers of religion, senior women, judges, servants, young girls. Then focus on 'Abigail's pack', the group of teenaged girls (addressed mostly as 'children' by the adults) who become the accusers of witches. What motivates them? How are they kept together and controlled by one strong personality? Are the others simply weak or gullible? See character notes on Abigail for further ideas.

Sharing common beliefs and values

Key Quotes

'There is either obedience or the church will burn like Hell is burning!' (Parris, p.35)

'... a person is either with this court or he must be counted against it, there be no road between.' (Danforth to Francis Nurse, p.85)

'Is there no good penitence but it be public?' (Proctor, pp.123–4)

How and why do communities accept and share common beliefs and values? A society cannot make laws to regulate its functioning unless there is some consensus on what is right and wrong which everyone will expect to see expressed in the laws.

When Hale asks the Proctors to recite the Ten Commandments, they need to demonstrate to him that their belief is deeper than rote-learning of the basic precepts in order to pass his test. Judge Danforth must insist that the community recognise, without question, the divine authority of his court's judgements to authorise executions of 'guilty' community members. And Proctor's confession must be seen to be public 'for the good instruction of the village' (Danforth, p.120).

Either/or debates about a professed fundamental belief can lead to a group's disagreement and fragmentation. Then the group is likely to split and 'factions' may develop to weaken authority's control, as Parris fears (p.35). In Salem's theocracy, the church Meeting House appropriately doubles as the courtroom because the two forces of law and order speak as one voice to maintain social cohesiveness, by suppressing questions and demonstrating public acquiescence to authority.

Conflict

Conflict, in Miller's play, is the inevitable flip-side of belonging in Salem's strained moral and social dynamics. This theme invites you to locate many different sites of conflict, trace apparent causes and consider how individuals respond in different ways to conflict.

KEY POINT

We can think of the following as a key legacy of America's Puritan origins: hanging on to a sense of being 'right', of having the 'truth' and defending hard-won ideological safety. Miller comments that modern America has inherited something of this deep sense of being right, of a belief that America must be protected as the 'New Jerusalem' in an evil cosmos (p.15).

Cosmic conflict: God versus the Devil

KEY QUOTES

'This is a sharp time, now, a precise time – we live no longer in the dusky afternoon when evil mixed itself with good and befuddled the world.' (Danforth, p.85)

'It is surely a stroke of hell upon you.' (Ann Putnam to Parris, p.21)

'Let you counsel among yourselves; think on your village and what may have drawn from heaven such thundering wrath upon you all.' (Hale, p.73)

'No man may longer doubt the powers of the dark are gathered in monstrous attack upon this village.' (Hale, p.62)

The seventeenth-century Puritan worldview saw the battle between God and the Devil for Christian souls as a titanic reality, made apparent to humans on earth in an ever-present spiritual conflict between good and evil. The vigilant Christian should take this cosmic or other-worldly conflict as a given and look to see it manifesting in many forms in everyday experience. As Miller points out, this is still not an uncommon belief today for many people, it is hugely influential in thinking about world events, and it requires careful examination as a reality-shaping idea.

Carefully read Miller's comprehensive notes (pp.37–40) when Hale, 'the eager-eyed intellectual', first arrives to confront 'the Fiend himself'. These notes link the Salem material with the ideological use of the Devil as a weapon to enforce public obedience, demonise political opposition and immorality, define Communist enemies in the Cold War and so on.

Spiritual conflict: the Devil and witches

Key Quotes

'How can it be the Devil? Why would he choose my house to strike? We have all manner of licentious people in the village!' (Parris, p.44)

'What victory would the Devil have to win a soul already bad? It is the best the Devil wants, and who is better than the minister?' (Hale, p.44)

'... the Devil is alive in Salem, and we dare not quail to follow wherever the accusing finger points!' (Hale to Francis Nurse, p.68)

'You have sent your spirit out upon this child, have you not? Are you gathering souls for the Devil?' (Hale to Tituba about Betty, p.46)

'She sends her spirit on me in church; she makes me laugh at prayer!' (Abigail, p.46)

'Mary Warren! Draw back your spirit out of them!' (Danforth, p.102)

The characters endure spiritual conflict in a number of ways. Some are to do with the apparent activities of the Devil and witches.

The (unintentional on their part) comic irony in the exchange between Parris and Hale – two ministers of God – is not lost on the audience (p.44). Parris complains of unfairness because the Devil ought to target lost souls in the village rather than him, and Hale – as yet untroubled by doubts – smugly asserts every minister's godly virtues.

In a witch-hunt, apparent spirituality and virtuous living are no protection – anyone may make accusation, and the onus is on named persons to prove themselves innocent or confess. Rebecca Nurse, charged with 'the marvellous and supernatural murder of Goody Putnam's babies' (p.67), can never prove herself innocent of an invisible crime; and her religious convictions and personal integrity prevent her from saving her life by making a false confession.

Similarly, anyone can claim to have been injured by another person directing malicious thoughts at them. Mary describes being attacked by such a spirit in court (p.57). Furthermore, 'Spectral evidence', the visible shape of the witch appearing to someone, was a contentious but permitted component of Salem trials (see transcripts for details). Abigail 'sees' Mary in changed shape as a dangerous 'yellow bird', while the real Mary is in plain view (p.101).

Spiritual conflict upsets the rational mind

KEY QUOTES

'There might also be a dragon with five legs in my house, but no one has ever seen it.' (Proctor, p.93)
'We are here, Your Honour, precisely to discover what no one has ever seen' (Parris, p.93)

Another form of spiritual conflict occurs within the individual who wants to be part of Salem's Christian community, yet whose rational mind rejects 'proof' that is unverifiable and insubstantial. Examples include the tenuous link between Rebecca Nurse and the dead Putnam children; merely circumstantial evidence like Martha Corey's books or Goody Good's mumbling; and superstitious suggestion, like the poppet stuck with a needle that condemns Elizabeth.

Proctor and Hale, in different ways, experience this kind of inner conflict about spirituality most deeply. If the Devil's spirits are invisible, how can you engage in conflict when you can't see your foe? Proctor's disbelief that 'unseen' things in his house could nonetheless be there articulates a rational person's frustration at the sort of infuriatingly cocksure statement Parris makes, that is so difficult to contest (p.93).

See also the theme of 'Bewilderment', discussed below.

Conflict within the community

KEY QUOTES

'I have often wondered if the Devil be in it somewhere; I cannot understand you people otherwise.' (Parris, p.34)
'This man is killing his neighbours for their land!' (Corey about Putnam, p.87)

If law and religion can stabilise and control a social group, they may equally be divisive in some instances, when individuals refuse to comply, challenge the authority of leaders, or persecute each other. Negative rumours, allegations and intimidation all unsettle a community and undermine relationships.

Look carefully at the key sequence (pp.32–6), which pinpoints a bitter division in Salem village. Proctor raises objections (after Rebecca has begged that they don't start arguing again) when Putnam instructs Parris how he will proceed with Hale. Parris has no aptitude as a Christian minister and little sympathy with the community. His demands irritate the farmers, leading Proctor to claim that there's not enough real spirituality to encourage people to attend church.

Dissatisfaction with spiritual practice under Parris collides fatally with quarrels about property rights. Putnam, Proctor, Corey and the Nurses are entangled in a dispute just as Hale walks in (p.36). This dispute is never resolved – it just finds a more destructive manifestation in the witch-hunt.

Tolerating diversity

Key quotes

'I may speak my heart, I think!' (Proctor, p.35)

'What, are we Quakers? We are not Quakers here yet, Mr Proctor.' (Parris, p.35)

Does any community have to set limits on absolute individual freedom? Why does a highly controlling society, like a theocracy, have to be especially vigilant about curbing its free-speakers? What kind of diversity is tolerated and how much: moral, sexual, religious, legal? The community depicted in *The Crucible* is one in which very little diversity is tolerated, and this in itself is seen by Miller to be a source of tension and conflict, unhealthy for the society as a whole.

Parris and Putnam join to accuse Proctor of leading like-minded 'followers' to make 'a faction and a party' against Parris (p.35). Proctor's reluctance to attend church and his insistence on his right to express his opinion are seen by Parris as subversive acts that threaten the community – and undermine his own authority.

Q Is Parris's participation in Danforth's inquisitorial court really just a self-serving attempt to salvage some local authority?

How is sexuality policed?

The sexual theme, and the notion of 'illicit sexuality', was something Miller noticed in almost every testimony he read: 'Had there been no tinder of guilt to set aflame, had the cult and culture of repression not ruled so tightly, no outbreak would have been possible' (*Timebends*, pp.340–1).

Look for situations in the play where sex as pleasure is usually outweighed by feelings of sin, shame and guilt. See Abigail's confession of what Tituba made her do (p.46) and read Miller's notes (pp.39–40).

This idea must be treated carefully but it is integral to the play's meaning. Miller notes that a process of societal 'cleansing' with identifiable sinners to be punished actually enables everyone in the community to undergo 'projection of one's own vileness onto others in order to wipe it out with their blood' (*Timebends*, p.337). He also notes in the record that the judges used to enjoy their court break times 'playing shovelboard with their holy adolescent witnesses and sharing an ale with them in the local tavern' (*Timebends*, p.341). Obviously this was not seen as improper behaviour for Puritans in the context of a battle between God and the Devil: Mary comments on it with defensive pride at her new status (p.59).

Domestic conflict

Key quotes

'I have gone tiptoe in this house all seven month since she is gone.' (Proctor, p.55)
'Suspicion kissed you when I did; I never knew how I should say my love. It were a cold house I kept!' (Elizabeth, p.119)

John and Elizabeth Proctor characterise key emotional tensions in a close relationship that has been fractured by adultery. Their capacity to recover trust is partly hampered by living in a sexually repressed society, where intimate conversation is awkward and always grounded in religious precepts. See the notes in Characters & Relationships for more points.

Parris's dysfunctional household expresses other tensions. Betty's semi-comatose state may be a way of evading interrogation by her minister father, who discovered her raising spirits in the wood with Abigail, coupled with unresolved grief for her dead mother. Tituba expresses a deep hatred of her master in her 'confession fantasy' of murdering him (p.48) and Abigail deceives, then finally robs, the weak uncle who has taken her in.

In another example, Giles Corey describes his own absurd petty conflict with Martha about her books, an anecdote that is blown out of all proportion and contributes to her being tried and executed.

Conflict within the individual

key quotes

'I come to do the Devil's work. I come to counsel Christians they should belie themselves ... There is blood on my head!' (Hale, p.114)

'What others say and what I sign to is not the same ... Because I lie and sign myself to lies!' (Proctor, p.124)

Several kinds of inner conflict can be traced in the play.

- One is related to telling lies to save your life. Several characters are encouraged to confess to something they know they didn't do (and that couldn't be done by humans at all, in fact) but the pay-off – not to lose their life – is worthwhile even though they have sacrificed their honesty and good name. Surely most people could allow themselves to live and accept that they're moral cowards if faced with this conflict of conscience? Some, like Rebecca, refuse, as does Elizabeth when Hale asks her if she believes in witches (p.66). Proctor tries to get away with it but Danforth's insistence finally drives him through compromise to a brave resolution of his conflict.

- Another kind of inner conflict is what Hale the rational minister experiences – because he compromises his own conscience and then encourages others to do the same. His inner spirituality ends up in shreds.

- Mary's terror of Abigail colliding with her desire to tell the truth sets up another kind of inner conflict, that leads to her wild breakdown in court (pp.101–4).

- Proctor's inner conflict is about who he considers himself to be as a person, and how harshly he judges himself for his sinfulness.

Children in an adult's community

key quotes

'A child's spirit is like a child, you can never catch it by running after it; you must stand still, and, for love, it will soon itself come back.' (Rebecca, p.32)

'Goody Ann! You sent a child to conjure up the dead?' (Rebecca to Mrs Putnam, p.42)

'We are what we always were in Salem, but now the little crazy children are jangling the keys of the kingdom, and common vengeance writes the law!' (Proctor, p.72)

'... the world goes mad, and it profit nothing you should lay the cause to the vengeance of a little girl.' (Hale to Proctor, p.73)

This theme opens up very sensitive issues in the play. Approach it from two perspectives, the adults' and the girls'.

Adults relating to children

Rebecca Nurse, with her large family, years of experience and gentle personality, has a calming influence on Betty. John Proctor, a father, agrees with Rebecca's no-fuss ideas about letting children go through their 'silly seasons' (p.32).

A distressing history of dead babies has made Ann Putnam resentful and suspicious – Rebecca's handling of Betty suggests some secret power beyond maternal know-how. Her guilty feelings are upset further when Rebecca expresses strong disapproval of Ann's sending Ruth Putnam to consult Tituba. Tituba is horrified to be accused of harming the girls at all: 'I don't desire to hurt little children' (p.47).

Danforth and other men in authority support and encourage the 'children' to fuel the court proceedings, yet have no understanding of how this teenage hysteria has been activated.

Q Danforth is especially resistant to criticising the 'saintly' child Abigail. Why do you think this is – because she's pretty? looks innocent or frightened? may see spirits that he can't see but that fill him with supernatural dread? could just as easily accuse him if he tries to stop her?

What motivates the girls?

Miller felt as appalled as we must to learn from historical documents that in the small Salem community, nineteen people were hanged, many others imprisoned and hundreds 'named', to say nothing of the disrupted world left behind, simply on the fantastic accusations of a small group of young girls. You'll find useful material in Miller's source Starkey (1949), Hansen (1969) and Hoffer (1996).

Abigail is motivated most obviously by hatred: she wants to murder her rival for John's love. Once the naming begins, the others follow her lead in self-defence, recognising safety in numbers to maintain the fiction and stimulate each other's fantasies. The result, as Miller depicts it, is mass-hysteria.

Bewilderment

The word 'bewilder' was first recorded around 1684 (*OED*), making it a new word at the time of the Salem witch trials and a very appropriate term to describe the kind of mental aberration depicted in the play.

It meant to be lost literally in pathless places or to be in a similar confused, lost state of mind. This was and still is a seriously upsetting situation to be in, especially for someone living in a society that prides itself on adhering to a clearly defined 'way' of being and discourages deviations, challenges or doubts. A number of characters in *The Crucible* experience bewilderment or accuse someone else of being bewildered at crucial moments. Some examples are:

- Elizabeth thinks John is 'somewhat bewildered' for lusting after Abigail (p.55).
- John warns Elizabeth that she will bewilder Hale by denying that witches exist (p.66).
- Danforth sarcastically tells Hale: 'for a man of such terrible learning you are most bewildered', when Hale tries to beg for proper lawyers to defend the accused – in Danforth's view, they're witches, so there will be no witnesses to their crimes, so who needs lawyers? (p.90).

Hysteria and cognitive dissonance

Two important psychological terms can be used to describe the characters' responses to challenges that threaten to 'bewilder' the mind: 'hysteria' and 'cognitive dissonance'.

Hysteria is often devalued as a temper tantrum but the medical term refers to a serious functional disturbance of the entire nervous system, often activated by severe stress or conflicting impulses. Mary Warren describes the classic onset of symptoms that mark her first hysterical episode in court: 'misty coldness', crawling flesh, a choking sensation, dissociation, 'a screamin' voice' then a realisation that the voice is her own (p.57). She isn't pretending when she falls into convulsions but the trigger is usually Abigail, who cues and activates panic in the others.

Earlier, Hale describes to Abigail precisely those feeling of strangeness or a 'sudden cold wind' heralding the presence of malign spirits (p.45), which she (consciously or unconsciously) reproduces when she puts herself into the hysterical trance, feeling cold to Hathorne's touch (p.96).

Unlike Mary, who can't even pretend to 'faint' on order, Abigail calculates the most effective moment to stage her hysterical visions of persecution. Is she always consciously manipulating the court, do you think? Does hysteria break out in her when the stress becomes intolerable?

The term **cognitive dissonance** describes the way people rationalise their actions by denying to themselves anything they've done that would go against the vision they want to preserve of themselves as people with certain qualities. Danforth is an example (although he mixes genuine cognitive dissonance with outright hypocrisy when he presses ahead with executions in spite of contrary advice). Hale looks back at the end with horror on his earlier cognitive dissonance, when he was acting as the destructive investigator for God. Elizabeth comes late to an admission of her faulty pride in plain virtue. Can you think of other examples?

Witchcraft, the Devil and bewilderment

There are many opportunities for bewilderment as the characters contemplate the existence of witches and the presence of the Devil in their midst.

- Do witches exist? How can people know?
- Proctor admits: 'I have no knowledge of it; the Bible speaks of witches, and I will not deny them' (to Hale, p.66); but Elizabeth, an upright Christian, declares: 'I cannot believe it ... I cannot think the Devil may own a woman's soul ... when she keeps an upright way' (p.66).
- Witches have the status of 'Biblical' truth, as in God's words to Moses: 'Thou shalt not suffer a witch to live' (Exodus 22:18). To literal-minded fundamentalists, then, both the existence of witches and the necessity of killing them are facts. But where is the proof finally? Is it enough to hang people?
- Persecution by unseen/unseeable enemies. This ensures maximum bewilderment because the Devil is an ever-present enemy to the mind and soul of everyone, breaking social stability, causing dissension and eroding a peaceful life. Rebecca's idea that they should look within themselves for what is upsetting the community has less dramatic clout than: 'The Devil's loose in Salem, Mr Proctor; we must discover where he's hiding (Mary, pp.58–9).

Words as weapons

Nowadays, most people feel comfortable (albeit to varying degrees) in using sexually charged, religious or violent phrases to express themselves, even about trivial things. Our casual dismissal of such strong words is quite the reverse of a situation where people are making serious accusations about, and being accused of, specific unseeable malevolence towards others by mumbling or cursing. Miller's play picks up the idea that every word matters because it may be seen to carry an intended meaning that can have a real physical effect in the world. Some gullible people believe this; others (like Proctor) dismiss it rationally as ludicrous.

- Notice how Hale reverts to Latin, the holy language of power for Christianity, when exorcising the Devil from Betty (p.44). Why should Latin be especially powerful?
- Proctor knows why he's been asked to sign his confession, which must be seen publicly to have the desired (by Parris and Danforth) effect (p.123).
- Are you one of us? Can you prove it? Can we trust your word? These are questions that people are forced to answer today in some situations by using particular formulaic words, like the Ten Commandments, oaths or prayers … what words of power do you know?
- The power of 'naming', even of being 'mentioned somewhat', is something that can impact on anyone, whether they are innocent or guilty. Look again at the HUAC blacklisting. Who has been mentioned somewhat in the recent news: can you identify some victims being set up in any one week?

Fear and courage

Key Quote

'I will fear nothing.' (Elizabeth, *with great fear*, p.72)

When we are afraid, the need to summon up courage is even more necessary and much harder to achieve.

- Elizabeth puts on a brave face as she's arrested but she has good reason to be afraid of Abigail's hold over the court.
- Hale points out that there is 'a prodigious fear of the court' that makes people reluctant to say their piece; Danforth interprets this as a sign not of his court's menacing approach but of the 'prodigious

guilt in the country' (p.88). For him, people are afraid of the court only because they're guilty. Proctor articulates his own fears about being believed in such a negative environment (p.66).

- Individuals who act in non-conforming ways require courage in highly controlled societies. Proctor says he would rather pray at home, partly because he dislikes Parris. Hale notes: 'Mr Proctor, your house is not a church; your theology must tell you that ... A Christian on Sabbath Day must be in church' (p.63).

Fear of what's beyond Salem's boundaries ... the wild

Miller notes that 'to the European world the whole province was a barbaric frontier inhabited by a sect of fanatics' (p.13). Yet early Puritans saw themselves as carrying the civilising light of Christianity in their communities. They were fearful of the land outside the defended settlements, full of savage Indians, untamed spaces, dense forests with wild animals – an unknown, 'unowned', godless wasteland. Abigail had seen her parents massacred by Indians.

There is a widespread fear of 'wildness' as the antithesis (opposite) of order, proper behaviour and morality. Note the significance of Parris stating that the girls were dancing 'like heathen in the forest' (p.19) – that is, outside the town, and committing acts that lie outside the socially-sanctioned boundaries of acceptable behaviour.

Reiteration of the word 'wild' occurs at crisis points to emphasise the absurdity or seriousness of what's being proposed, seen or decided. Examples include:

- Proctor calls Abigail's talk wild – she says she is wild and may say wild things (p.29).
- Putnam retorts to Proctor about who owns the forest: 'Why, we are surely gone wild this year. What anarchy is this?' (p.36).
- Elizabeth says: 'The town's gone wild, I think' (p.53) with the court and witch trials.
- Elizabeth again to Hale: 'They've surely gone wild now, Mr Hale!' (p.67) when they hear of Rebecca's arrest.
- Hale describes Mary's terrified fit as 'this child's gone wild' (p.104).

Troubled souls are fearful

Miller notes that: 'These people had no ritual for the washing away of sins' (p.27), no confession with penance and absolution, like the old

Catholic tradition. Individual conscience must keep a person honest. Public confessions are useful for serious crimes because they instruct the community.

Ironically, the souls in terror at the end are not those of the people about to be executed but of the ministers who need to justify their own reprehensible acts by extracting confessions from the people they've condemned. Without these confessions, 'doubts are multiplied, many honest people will weep for them, and our good purpose is lost in their tears' (Parris to Danforth, p.112).

Striving

If you browbeat a victim with questioning until they make a confession, it justifies your ideological correctness, the truth of your truth, doesn't it? If you fail, you are likely to be condemned as soft, not committed enough or open later to the charge of being unjust if the victim retaliates. HUAC and Salem judges both knew how to break down stubborn opponents, with the reward of a justified confession.

The term 'striving' is most often connected with the Chinese Cultural Revolution era, when opponents were forcibly harangued by the Red Guard in public until their minds submitted. Miller tells of meeting a Chinese writer who had been in solitary confinement for years, then was released in 1979 and saw a production of *The Crucible* in Shanghai. She told Miller: 'I looked at the play and thought, how could he have known the Chinese situation?' (cited in Gussow, p.88).

Danforth's solution to the tricky moral situation in Act 4 (nobody's confessed) is to choose the supposedly weakest person and try to break them: he asks Parris 'which of these in your opinion may be brought to God? I will myself strive with him till dawn' (p.112). This is an exercise in cynical self-protection, not for the good of prisoners' souls.

Other 'striving' moments you should explore further:
- Hale strives with the Devil for confessions (Act 1).
- Hale strives with the Proctors about theological correctness (Act 2).
- Hathorne strives with Mary Warren about fainting (Act 3).
- Danforth strives with Elizabeth for the truth about Proctor and Abigail (Act 3).

- Danforth strives with Abigail – she wins (Act 3).
- Parris, Hale and Danforth strive to get confessions from the condemned (Act 4).

Judgement and justice

Key Quotes

'Mr Hale, you surely do not doubt my justice.' (Danforth, p.89)

'I should hang ten thousand that dared to rise against the law, and an ocean of salt tears could not melt the resolution of the statutes.' (Danforth, p.113)

'... I cannot withhold from them the perfection of their punishment.' (Danforth, 114)

Hale is keen to apply theological arguments and obtain confessions; he quickly sees, however, that the Salem courtroom is not interested in dispensing justice but in imposing judgement. Deputy-Governor Danforth's court of *Oyer and Terminer* ('hear and determine') is a specially convened criminal hearing in Salem, but his dominating control of procedures and selective admission of evidence weigh strongly against fair hearings for anyone accused.

In this society, the Bible is the basis for the law. Danforth spells it out in court for the girls and for the play's audience (p.92).

God's justice

Key Quote

'Let you fear nothing! Another judgement waits us all!' (Rebecca, p.125)

Rebecca goes to death bravely because she has faith in God's fair judgement. Her words infuriate Danforth by denying him the high moral ground.

Judging each other

Key Quotes

'I cannot speak but I am doubted, every moment judged for lies, as though I come into a court when I come into this house!' (Proctor, p.55)

'The magistrate sits in your heart that judges you.' (Elizabeth to Proctor, p.55)

Focus on how John and Elizabeth argue their way to self-confession and then non-judgemental understanding with loving forgiveness.

Charity

> 'I have broke charity with the woman ...' (Giles Corey, p.79)
> 'No, you cannot break charity with your minister.' (Rebecca to Proctor, p.35)

Greek and Latin use several words to indicate different kinds of love. 'Eros' refers to sexual desire; 'philia' to loving friendship; 'agape' or 'caritas', charity, to patient caring love for fellow humans. The play shows a catastrophic failure of charity in the Salem community.

Christians say 'God is Love', yet the religion can be stern and punitive in a theocracy, where the experience of joy must be repressed, knowledge curbed and sexual energy sublimated into hard work and obedience to the demands of the Meeting House. The harmony of belonging is maintained by acceptance of faults and the exercising of charity – that is, care, concern, understanding, loving forgiveness, tolerance and acceptance. Salem's mode of controlling 'harmony' is punitive and retributive (uncharitable and vengeful). Hale, too, has broken charity as a minister by urging people to lie and live.

Failure of friendships

> 'There is a misty plot afoot so subtle we should be criminal to cling to old respects and ancient friendships.' (Hale, p.68)
> 'I have three children – how may I teach them to walk like men in the world, and I sold my friends?' (Proctor, p.124)

Rebecca thinks that Proctor, by confessing, may appear to have betrayed their friendship: 'Oh, John – God send his mercy on you' (p.121).

Is it permissible to break confidences? The court raises this question when Giles Corey says his evidence against Putnam has been told in confidence and he can't reveal his source (pp.87–8). Parris seizes on the point – he sees secrets as incriminatory, indicative of a faction to bring him down (p.88). However, our sympathies are with Giles – his wife is already condemned and anyone he names will be arrested, too.

The issue of 'breaking charity' became serious for Miller in the 1950s when old friends like Elia Kazan were called to testify before HUAC. Miller notes the distrust that replaced friendship and fractured kind and decent people's respect for each other. He writes:

I was experiencing a bitterness with the country that I had never even imagined before, a hatred of its stupidity and its throwing away of its freedom. Who or what was now safer because this man in his human weakness had been forced to humiliate himself? What truth had been enhanced by all this anguish? (*Timebends*, p.334)

DIFFERENT INTERPRETATIONS

Different interpretations arise from different responses to a text. Over time, a text will give rise to a wide range of responses from its readers, who may come from various social or cultural groups and live in very different places and historical periods. These responses can be published in newspapers, journals and books by critics and reviewers, or they can be expressed in discussions among readers in the media, classrooms, book groups and so on. While there is no single correct reading or interpretation of a text, it is important to understand that an interpretation is more than an 'opinion' – it is the justification of a point of view on the text. To present an interpretation of the text based on your point of view you must use a logical argument and support it with relevant evidence from the text.

The play's reception

The initial audience reception and reviews of *The Crucible* were not positive. Miller recalls the reaction of the audience on opening night, 22 January 1953:

> I had not quite bargained for ... the hostility in the New York audience as the theme of the play was revealed; an invisible sheet of ice formed over their heads, thick enough to skate on.
> (*Timebends*, p.347)

This response implies a view of the play as overtly political, and of its meaning as relating chiefly to the HUAC hearings. However, the reviewer for the *New York Times*, Brooks Atkinson, saw *The Crucible* not as 'pleading a case in dramatic form' but as 'a self-contained play about a terrible period in American history' (Atkinson 1953). Nevertheless, Atkinson saw it as having 'considerable pertinence for today' but lacking the universality of Miller's previous (and hugely successful) play, *Death of a Salesman*.

Over time, though, audiences did not make the political connection as directly, and became more appreciative of the play as a dramatic work that could convey larger, more universal themes. Indeed, just two years later an off-Broadway production in New York ran for two years, and

Miller notes that the 'metaphor of the immortal underlying forces that can always rise again was now an admissible thing for the press to consider' (*Timebends*, p.348).

Later again, at a London production in 1965, Miller overheard a remark that the play 'had something to do with that American senator – what was his name?'; for Miller, this was evidence that the play had 'now become art, cut from its roots, a spectacle of human passions purely' (*Timebends*, p.349). *The Crucible* eventually became Miller's most performed play, both in the United States and internationally.

Interpreting Abigail

The above overview suggests that one source of different interpretations of *The Crucible* is the extent to which we see it purely as a political statement on contemporary (that is, 1950s) events in the United States. Is this the real source of the play's meaning and significance? Or are the events in Salem in 1692 meaningful and significant in and of themselves? Or is it really a play about human passions and motivations that are timeless and universal? A balanced reading needs to take all of these factors into consideration, but there is considerable scope for placing different weight on each.

Another source of different interpretations is the view we take of individual characters. How sympathetically do we ultimately view John Proctor? Or Reverend Hale? Or the 'crazy children'? Who is the central character: Proctor? or is it really Abigail, whose actions and desires drive so much of the drama? In a live production, our response to characters depends critically on the actors' performances, which can bring out complexities though facial expressions, gestures, silences, vocal tone and so on. However, just focusing on the text alone can generate quite different viewpoints on the characters. The following discussion of Abigail shows how it is possible to take contrasting, yet equally well-supported, views of her role.

Interpretation 1: Abigail is the real villain of the play.

Abigail is malicious, a liar, a thief and (by default) a murderess of people condemned to die by her testimony. She is also one of the few characters who actually engages in an act of 'witchcraft': she 'drank a charm to kill

Goody Proctor' (p.26). Yet she leads the girls who point their fingers at others, not caring who might live or die as long as the girls remain free.

Her falling like 'a struck beast' and having a needle stuck 'two inches in the flesh of her belly' are clearly staged (p.70), part of the plan she devises in cold blood to frame Elizabeth Proctor while watching Mary making the poppet in court.

When Proctor's confession of adultery leads Hale to seriously question her character and testimony, Abigail stages another performance, claiming to see Mary's spirit in the form of a 'yellow bird' (p.101). It is an idea that she has clearly taken from Hale's initial questioning, when he suggested that a person's spirit can take the form of a 'bird invisible to others' (p.44). Although Hale is clearly not taken in, Abigail's performance – backed up by Mercy and Susanna – is so compelling that not only are Parris and Danforth convinced she is genuine, but Mary recants and declares Proctor 'the Devil's man' (p.104).

Other characters commit appalling acts, condemning innocent people to hang, yet they do so out of a commitment to principles and values, such as Danforth's commitment to judicial process or Hale's to his religious convictions. The Putnams do act maliciously, blaming Rebecca Nurse for the deaths of their children, yet they are relatively minor players in the unfolding drama, and at least seem to believe that, however improbably, Rebecca is somehow responsible. Abigail, though, cruelly and deliberately manipulates others to her own ends, never expressing any remorse or sense of morality. She is at the centre of it all, and is the real villain of the play.

Interpretation 2: Abigail is more a victim than a villain.

It would be difficult to argue a completely contrary case for Abigail, or to excuse the damage she does. However, there are strong grounds for feeling sympathetic towards Abigail and even for seeing her as one more of the play's victims, caught up in larger forces that she can do little to control.

She is essentially at the mercy of the men who surround her. She is certainly a willing participant in her affair with Proctor, but she is far more hurt by it than he is. She loses not only her lover, but her job; he returns to his marriage and family, showing no further concern for Abigail's welfare. She is then caught up in accusations of witchcraft, investigations that are carried out by a series of men – Parris, Hale, Danforth – who have the power to jail and even execute her. In this threatening situation, Abigail clings to the only form of power available to her, which is to name others as witches and represent herself as one who is resisting the lures of Satan.

She has, of course, behaved foolishly: her affair with Proctor could never lead to happiness; she has danced naked in the forest which she knows is forbidden. However, the severe restrictions imposed on her (as a child and as a female) by this patriarchal society mean that the consequences of these actions are extremely harsh. Faced with a night in the stocks, or jail, she seeks to take control of her life. Unfortunately, to do so, she is forced to take a series of increasingly desperate measures.

As the trials proceed, the likely punishment if Abigail is found to be deliberately misleading the court becomes more and more serious. This in turn places her under enormous strain. She may well be acting when she falls to the floor as if in response to a needle in a poppet (as recounted in Act 2), but her *utter conviction* in Act 3, when she talks to the yellow bird and behaves *as though hypnotized* (p.102), could easily be something more genuine. Abigail would certainly be terrified of the consequences of being found to be lying at this point: her life is at stake, and if she believes she sees a yellow bird, and feels compelled to repeat Mary's words, it is because these seem the only possibilities for survival left to her.

Abigail makes poor choices, and acts with callous disregard for others. Yet she is also a victim of the society in which she lives, which demands that she is submissive, humble and compliant, when she is none of these things. Her initial crimes are simply to seek independence and to defy male authority: these are understandable. She seeks to take control over her life, but the only people who can control her fate are the men who surround her, who use her for their own purposes and are more concerned with upholding the institutions of religion and law than with the wellbeing of a teenaged girl. In the end, Abigail is left with no family and no prospects, an outcome due partly to her own actions and partly to the nature of her society, which allows her few rights, and even fewer freedoms.

A note on the film version

Miller collaborated on the screenplay for the 1996 film version, directed sensitively (some say unimaginatively) by theatre professional, Nicholas Hytner. The film's focus is on the crucially flawed emotional triangle of Abigail (Winona Ryder), John Proctor (Daniel Day-Lewis) and Elizabeth Proctor (Joan Allen), and how religious justice in the form of Danforth (Paul Scofield) interprets human action in the world. Despite the star cast and the focus on character and plot so typical of mainstream Hollywood cinema, Hytner's direction ensures that the film largely retains the play's shape and ambience. It is very worth watching because it conveys an unsettling sense of the claustrophobic and alienated frontier world of the Salem theocracy, especially as that kind of repressive patriarchy affects couple relationships, some men, and the lives of all women, young and old.

QUESTIONS & ANSWERS

This section focuses on your own analytical writing on the text, and gives you strategies for producing high quality responses in your coursework and exam essays.

Essay writing – an overview

An essay is a formal and serious piece of writing that presents your point of view on the text, usually in response to a given essay topic. Your 'point of view' in an essay is your interpretation of the meaning of the text's language, structure, characters, situations and events, supported by detailed analysis of textual evidence.

Analyse – don't summarise

In your essays it is important to avoid simply summarising what happens in a text:

- A summary is a description or paraphrase (retelling in different words) of the characters and events. For example: 'Macbeth has a horrifying vision of a dagger dripping with blood before he goes to murder King Duncan'.
- An analysis is an explanation of the real meaning or significance that lies 'beneath' the text's words (and images, for a film). For example: 'Macbeth's vision of a bloody dagger shows how deeply uneasy he is about the violent act he is contemplating – as well as his sense that supernatural forces are impelling him to act'.

A limited amount of summary is sometimes necessary to let your reader know which part of the text you wish to discuss. However, always keep this to a minimum and follow it immediately with your analysis (explanation) of what this part of the text is really telling us.

Plan your essay

Carefully plan your essay so that you have a clear idea of what you are going to say. The plan ensures that your ideas flow logically, that your argument remains consistent and that you stay on the topic. An essay plan should be a list of **brief dot points** – no more than half a page. It includes:

- your central argument or main contention – a concise statement (usually in a single sentence) of your overall response to the topic. See 'Analysing a sample topic' for guidelines on how to formulate a main contention.

- three or four dot points for each paragraph indicating the main idea and evidence/examples from the text. Note that in your essay you will need to expand on these points and analyse the evidence.

Structure your essay

An essay is a complete, self-contained piece of writing. It has a clear beginning (the introduction), middle (several body paragraphs) and end (the last paragraph or conclusion). It must also have a central argument that runs throughout, linking each paragraph to form a coherent whole.

See examples of introductions and conclusions in the 'Analysing a sample topic' and 'Sample answer' sections.

The introduction establishes your overall response to the topic. It includes your main contention and outlines the main evidence you will refer to in the course of the essay. Write your introduction *after* you have done a plan and *before* you write the rest of the essay.

The body paragraphs argue your case – they present evidence from the text and explain how this evidence supports your argument. Each body paragraph needs:

- a strong topic sentence (usually the first sentence) that states the main point being made in the paragraph
- evidence from the text, including some brief quotations
- analysis of the textual evidence explaining its significance and explanation of how it supports your argument
- links back to the topic in one or more statements, usually towards the end of the paragraph.

Connect the body paragraphs so that your discussion flows smoothly. Use some linking words and phrases like 'similarly' and 'on the other hand', though don't start every paragraph like this. Another strategy is to use a significant word from the last sentence of one paragraph in the first sentence of the next.

Use key terms from the topic – or similes for them – throughout, so the relevance of your discussion to the topic is always clear.

The conclusion ties everything together and finishes the essay. It includes strong statements that emphasise your central argument and provide a clear response to the topic.

Avoid simply restating the points made earlier in the essay – this will end on a very flat note and imply that you have run out of ideas and vocabulary. The conclusion is meant to be a logical extension of what you have written, not just a repetition or summary of it. Writing an effective conclusion can be a challenge. Try using these tips:

- Start by linking back to the final sentence of the second-last paragraph – this helps your writing to 'flow', rather than just leaping back to your main contention straight away.
- Use similes and expressions with equivalent meanings to vary your vocabulary. This allows you to reinforce your line of argument without being repetitive.
- When planning your essay, think of one or two broad statements or observations about the text's wider meaning. These should be related to the topic and your overall argument. Keep them for the conclusion, since they will give you something 'new' to say but still follow logically from your discussion. The introduction will be focused on the topic, but the conclusion can present a wider view of the text.

Essay topics

The essay topics below show a range of possible styles and formats, and are suitable for senior English assessment tasks and examinations.

1 "… one can only pity them all, just as we shall be pitied some day."
   To what extent do we feel pity for the characters in *The Crucible*?

2 "… the balance has yet to be struck between order and freedom."
   'In *The Crucible*, the problems in Salem are caused by too much order and too little individual freedom.' Discuss.

3 "What profit him to bleed?"
   Do the executions achieve anything?

4 'There are no heroes or villains in the play – just individuals with human strengths and weaknesses.'
   Do you agree?

5 Reverend Hale says: "There is blood on my head!"
   How responsible is Hale for the deaths of innocent people?

6 'Danforth is as true to his conscience as John Proctor or Rebecca

Nurse are.'

Do you agree?

7 'The play shows that fear is at the heart of conflict.' Discuss.

8 'The way in which the characters respond to conflict shows us who is worthy of our admiration, and who is not.' Discuss.

9 'The characters struggle to balance the obligations of belonging to a group with their personal desires and beliefs.' Discuss.

10 'The Crucible suggests that we cannot have strong personal values unless we also have a strong sense of belonging to a group.' Discuss.

11 How does Miller's commentary impact on our understanding of the play's larger meaning?

Vocabulary for writing on The Crucible

Allegory: a story that has a double meaning: a surface, literal meaning; and a second, implied meaning. In The Crucible, the historical events depicted can be understood both in their own terms and as a reflection of, and commentary on, the HUAC 'witch-hunt' of Communists in the 1950s. The adjective allegorical might also be useful in your writing.

Cognitive dissonance: a tension within a person caused by their holding two contradictory ideas or beliefs simultaneously; they rationalise their actions by denying anything that goes against their view of themselves, their beliefs and values etc.

Duologue: conversation between two characters, e.g. John and Elizabeth Proctor in Act 2.

HUAC: the House Un-American Activities Committee, a powerful US committee in the 1940s and 1950s, but which then lost prestige in the 1960s. The Crucible implies a parallel between the interrogation of named individuals in Salem and the interrogation of suspected Communist spies and sympathisers by HUAC.

Hysteria: a serious disturbance of the entire nervous system, often activated by severe stress or conflicting impulses. In The Crucible the behaviour of the girls can be described as 'group hysteria'; Mary's breakdown at the end of Act 3 is also an example.

McCarthyism: term deriving from the activities and views of Senator Joseph McCarthy, who led anti-Communist feelings and paranoia in the US in the early 1950s; now used more widely to refer to unsubstantiated public accusations of disloyalty.

Theocracy: a system of government that sees a god or deity as the supreme ruler ('theo' is from the Greek word for god); religious leaders have substantial if not total power; for the Massachusetts theocracy in *The Crucible*, the Christian God is society's ruler and the Bible is the most authoritative text.

Analysing a sample topic

'The play shows that fear is at the heart of conflict.' Discuss.

Look carefully at the key terms: 'fear', 'at the heart' and 'conflict'. Although it looks like a simple statement, there are underlying complexities. What kind of conflict – the conflict between people? between different beliefs and values? within an individual? And fear of what – something real (pain, unhappiness, death)? or something imagined (the Devil, spells, witchcraft)?

Another issue to address is the meaning of the expression 'at the heart'. This is a figure of speech – obviously, conflict does not have a real, physical 'heart' – so you need to interpret this expression in a way that allows you to talk about the link between fear and conflict as it is explored in the play. Think about how you might paraphrase the topic: 'fear is the main cause of conflict', and 'fear is the essential factor in any conflict', are just two of many possibilities.

Once you have paraphrased the topic, decide if you agree or disagree with it. If you disagree, you might argue that fear is one of many causes but not the *main* cause; or that some conflict can occur without fear so fear is not *essential* to conflict. Clearly, the way you interpret 'at the heart of' will be crucial to how you frame your response to the topic and, in turn, your overall argument or main contention.

Implied in this topic is a comparison between fear and other causes of conflict. What else causes conflict in *The Crucible*? The Putnams' desire for more land could be one factor; the commitment to core beliefs and principles might be another. You might see fear as just one of a number of factors – and not necessarily 'at the heart' of conflict. Or you might see fear as the 'common denominator' that underlies all these other factors, and therefore very much the central element.

In the outline below, the response argues in agreement with the topic statement; the main contention or argument is stated in the final sentence of the introduction.

Sample introduction

> *The Crucible* presents a range of conflicts: within families and between families; between individuals and within individuals. Sometimes these conflicts involve desires for real, material objects, such as money or land. Other conflicts involve abstract concepts that cannot be seen or tested, such as a person's spirit or the Devil. Underlying all of these factors is the basic human emotion of fear: fear of the unknown, of isolation and rejection, of death, and – for some – of what lies beyond death.

Body paragraph 1

- Consider conflicts over land. Miller's comments (pp.31–2) point to the significance of these disputes. Link these considerations to your argument about fear.
- Look at the exchange between Putnam and Proctor (p.36).
- The struggle to make a living from the land is conveyed by Proctor at the start of Act 2 – farming is hard work with few rewards and no guarantee of success.
- Underlying this conflict over land is fear of hardship and poverty: farmers need every resource they can get because survival is so tenuous in this 'space so antagonistic to man' (p.15).

Body paragraph 2

- Other conflicts between individuals, e.g. Elizabeth and John Proctor, or Hale and Danforth, have different causes, but fear is still an underlying factor.
- Elizabeth and John face the deterioration of their marriage and further emotional pain. Tension between them is caused by John's betrayal, and their care and restraint with each other in Act 2 (*'holding back a full condemnation of her'*, p.53; *'fearing to anger him'*, p.54) show their fear that things might become worse.
- Hale and Danforth clash over their view of the girls' testimony: this conflict is heightened as both fear the consequences of the other getting their way. Danforth fears the loss of the court's authority and of his own status; he also shows a genuine fear of the Devil's presence in Salem (*'now he is frightened; there is real tension in his*

voice', p.101). Hale emerges as the more sincere as his biggest fear is of causing the loss of an innocent life – a fear that is realised.

Body paragraph 3

- For some of those who are named, fear of death is enough to drive them to confess. However, the refusal of some to confess – especially those who are widely respected – intensifies the conflict in the community and increases the stakes for all.
- For Rebecca Nurse, the main focus is on her soul. To confess is to condemn her to suffering not in this life but the next one: 'Another judgement waits us all!' (p.125).
- When Proctor refuses to confess publicly, Rebecca cries 'Let you fear nothing' (p.125) – that is, if we act well in our lives then we have nothing to fear in the afterlife.
- Hale, however, knows he has done the wrong thing, and fears the consequences for his soul: he believes there is 'blood on [his] head' for the deaths of innocent people, yet 'damnation's doubled on a minister who counsels men to lie' (pp.114, 115). This is Hale's inner conflict, which has fear, as well as guilt, at the centre of it.

Sample conclusion

Fear is at the heart of conflict in *The Crucible*, shaping the actions and decisions of all characters. Their fears might not always be obvious: other factors, such as greed, emotional tensions or a commitment to deeply held beliefs, might seem to be the motivating forces that bring people into conflict with one another. Underlying these, however, is the element of fear, which reflects in turn the extreme vulnerability of individuals in a new society, in a new world, surrounded in every way – physical as well as metaphysical – by the unfamiliar, the unknown and the unknowable.

SAMPLE ANSWER

"... the balance has yet to be struck between order and freedom." 'In *The Crucible*, the problems in Salem are caused by too much order and too little individual freedom.' Discuss.

As Miller suggests in his introductory comments to the play, the theocracy in Salem developed to ensure the stability and unity of this frontier society, but it also veered towards excessive regulation, repressing individual freedoms. When people did act with more freedom, a 'panic set in among all classes' and a strong reaction occurred to re-establish order. *The Crucible* illustrates the problems that result when society's authorities impose too much order and severely limit individual freedoms. Proctor and Abigail learn that, in such a world, to act in accordance with one's desires, or consistent with one's beliefs, leads to death. Abigail, too, steps outside the boundaries of accepted behaviour only to find that her options become increasingly narrow and extreme. Danforth and Hale represent the theocracy's leaders, one civil and one religious: both stand for order, due process and respect for the law (especially God's law). Their rigid application of these principles leads, tragically, to the execution of good and innocent people, and the almost complete breakdown of Salem society.

Proctor's most obvious act of individual freedom is his affair with Abigail, an act that breaks one of the Ten Commandments and places a severe strain on his marriage. However, Proctor expresses his individuality in other ways that are much less destructive, yet are still questioned by authority figures. He attends church infrequently due to his dislike of Parris's sermons, which he claims are only about 'hellfire and damnation'. Hale finds Proctor's non-attendance a fault, like his inability to name all ten of the Commandments. In fact, Proctor has helped to build the church, and resents that Parris has wasted money on golden candlesticks. We respect Proctor for these things, yet increasingly the expression of a personal viewpoint places him at odds with authority figures. Finally, Proctor seeks to expose the fraudulent testimony of the girls, which results in his being arrested and condemned to hang – the ultimate deprivation of his individual freedom.

Abigail rebels against the established order in several ways, yet she finds herself compelled to act as an instrument of the court. Her individuality is repressed and she performs in accordance with what the authority figures wish to see and hear. For this conformity, she retains her liberty, despite the damning evidence Proctor and Mary Warren bring against her. Yet at the end Abigail too is defeated, forced to flee Salem when it becomes apparent that she can have no future there.

Rebecca Nurse expresses a different kind of individual freedom – the freedom to live true to her beliefs and values. The court requires her to confess as part of its attempts to re-establish the social order; but Rebecca refuses, believing that a false confession would endanger her soul. Both Rebecca and Proctor have strong religious convictions and beliefs, which they hold in quite personal ways independent of what they are told by a minister – especially by Parris, whom they feel free to question and disagree with. Parris, however, grants them no such freedom: 'are we Quakers here?' he asks scornfully of Proctor, when the latter declares he is free to speak his heart. Rebecca and Proctor are hanged at the play's conclusion when they remain true to their personal beliefs rather than submit to the demands of authorities.

Deputy-Governor Danforth and Reverend Hale come into the fractured society of Salem and seek to impose order upon it. They take the Bible as the source of all truth and the basis of all law, and work to fit everything they see and hear in Salem into that rigid framework. Hale comes to realise that not only is this process flawed, but it actually leads to an increase in conflict and social breakdown. Danforth, though, insists on the validity of the judicial process, seeing this as the only way to reconcile differences and restore order. Like Parris, Danforth cannot accommodate individual variations, and much of the complexity of human motivation – such as what compels Elizabeth to lie to him, or what makes Abigail 'see' the yellow bird – appears to escape his comprehension. For Danforth, 'a person is either with this court or he must be counted against it': the imposition of order is a black-and-white affair that erases the individual and recognises only the group.

By the time Proctor and Rebecca are 'marked to hang', the form of 'order' that results from the witch trials is shown to be closer to a form of chaos. Hale states that 'there are orphans wandering from house to house' and 'the stink of rotting crops hangs everywhere'. It is not order, but disorder, that now characterises Salem. Those in authority have repressed individual freedoms to ensure social cohesion, but they have overlooked the need for freedom in any cohesive society. Individuals must follow the rules of the group, but they must also remain true to themselves in order to form the bonds that hold society together: the bonds of marriage, family and friendship. These bonds are severed by the excess of order in *The Crucible*, and the resulting problems destroy not only individual lives, but also – paradoxically – the theocracy itself.

REFERENCES & READING

The text

Miller, Arthur 2000 (1953), *The Crucible*, Penguin, London.

References and further reading

Atkinson, Brooks 1953, 'The Crucible', review, *The New York Times*, 23 January.

Gussow, Mel 2002, *Conversations with Miller*, Nick Hern Books, London.

Hansen, C. 1969, *Witchcraft at Salem*, George Braziller, New York.

Hoffer, P.C. 1996, *The Devil's Disciples. Makers of the Salem witchcraft trials*, Johns Hopkins U.P., Baltimore & London. (See especially Chapters 1, 2, 4, 5 and 7.)

Martine, J.J. 1979, *Critical Essays on Arthur Miller*, G. K. Hall & Co, Boston, Massachusetts.

See especially Thomas E. Porter, 'The Long Shadow of the Law: The Crucible' on 'the courtroom drama' and implications for American ideas of justice in the historical relationship between church and courthouse; and Robert A. Martin, 'Arthur Miller's The Crucible: Background and Sources'.

Miller, A. 1987, *Timebends. A Life*, Methuen, London.

— 1996, 'Why I wrote *The Crucible*: An Artist's Answer to politics', *The New Yorker*, 21 October, www.honors.umd.edu/HONR269J/archive/MillerCrucible.html

O'Reilly, K. 1983, *Hoover and the Un-Americans. The FBI, HUAC, and the Red Menace*, Temple U.P., Philadelphia. (See especially Ch.3, 'Shaping Public Opinion'.)

Schrecker, E. 1994, *The Age of McCarthyism: A brief history with documents*, St Martin's Press, Boston.

Starkey, M. 1949, *The Devil in Massachusetts*, New York.

Film

The Crucible 1996, Twentieth Century Fox, dir. Nicholas Hytner, screenplay by Arthur Miller. Starring Daniel Day-Lewis, Winona Ryder and Paul Scofield.

Good Night, and Good Luck 2005, dir. George Clooney, Warner Bros.

Set in 1953, when popular American TV presenter Ed Murrow took on McCarthy. Includes useful documentary footage of McCarthy and Roy Cohn conducting HUAC hearings.

An Enemy of the People 1978, dir. George Shaefer, Warner Bros. Starring Steve McQueen.

A close adaptation of Ibsen's play about a doctor who dares to challenge his community.

Websites

Beware the many essays and 'gradesaver' notes on this play: they are full of inaccuracies. Take time to make your own detailed notes and think through ideas.

Access very useful archives with maps, trial transcripts, biographies of individuals, etc. by searching for 'Salem Witch Trials'. A selection I found useful follows:

www.salemwitchtrials.com

An extensive archive of original material Miller would have read in some form as background research for play.

www.cnn.com/2005/SHOWBIZ/books/02/11/obit.miller/

Obituary for Arthur Miller.

news.bbc.co.uk/onthisday/hi/dates/stories/august/7/
newsid_2946000/2946420.stm

Short article on Miller and HUAC, 1958: Arthur Miller cleared of contempt (photo with Monroe).

www.evesmag.com/murrow.htm

A personal memoire of Edward R. Murrow by Joseph Wershba, CBS News, a journalist colleague and friend. Important parallels with things Proctor says about how to be a good model to children, paralysing effects of fear, the right to speak out, integrity of courts, individual's responsibility for society. Inspiring words from brave broadcasters who went against McCarthy at a time when society was paralysed by fear of naming and blacklisting.

www.pbs.org/newshour/bb/entertainment/july-dec97/blacklist_10-24.html

'Seeing Red': a NewsHour transcript of an interview with Hollywood blacklisted artists.

www.writing.upenn.edu/~afilreis/50s/menace-emerges.html

Ellen Schrecker, 'Communism and National Security: The Menace emerges', Ch.3 from The Age of McCarthyism.

www.washingtonpost.com/wp-srv/style/longterm/review96/cruciblerose.htm

Review by Lloyd Rose of Nicholas Hytner's film of The Crucible.